MEAN GIRL NO MORE

How to Shift from Sabotage to Support and

Build a Powerful Inner Circle

PEGGY VASQUEZ

OTHER BOOKS BY PEGGY VASQUEZ

Not, "Just an Admin"

This book is dedicated to my inner circle
for without you I would still be dreaming
of becoming the woman I was meant to be.

CONTENTS

Foreword

Whenever I introduce Peggy Vasquez on stage, I precede her name with the word 'inimitable'. It means unique, special, not to be imitated.

Peggy always sees things with wisdom that brings instant clarity to complex subjects. She is never scared to tackle difficult issues and anyone who has seen her keynote will testify to the life-changing nature of her message. I was beyond excited therefore, when she asked me to read this, her second book, and to write the foreword.

It didn't disappoint. This is a book that I wish someone had taken the initiative and courage to write well before now. I have a feeling that countless women, all over the world, will be spared the angst and hurt that most of us, if we are honest, have been through at one stage or another at the hands of the 'mean girls' that enter our lives--because of Peggy's determination to lift the lid on behaviors that are whispered about behind closed doors but never addressed.

These insidious, undermining, and competitive incidents that most of us encounter many times in our working lives as women are learned behaviors from the cradle. We're taught to compete for attention and to value ourselves based on how others see us. Peggy has redefined these myths and seeks to encourage us on a journey of self-exploration and discovery of our true value and worth.

Through a series of brave, relatable, real-life stories, she uncovers the truth behind these negative behaviors and shows us how to build a powerful inner circle that will raise our conviction in our own abilities and the confidence to follow our dreams.

This book is packed with practical tips and exercises as well as a huge dose of inspiration. Peggy is a role model for every woman that wants to live their best life through lifting others, not destroying them.

Like her keynote speeches, you will find this book both life-changing and life-affirming. Peggy Vasquez lives her message and is the real deal. I for one am honored to be part of her inner circle.

Lucy Brazier

CEO, Marcham Publishing, Publisher of Executive Secretary Magazine

CHAPTER**ONE**

Mean Girls

There you are, the new girl in the office, trying to find your place with your executive and fit into the culture and office dynamic. But a female co-worker rebuffs your every attempt to be friendly. She purposely leaves you out of office parties, lunches, and barbecues.

Even your birthday was pointedly ignored. You keep trying to be professional and cheerful, but instead of friendship, you are handed coldness, bullying, and even outright sabotage of your business projects. You're constantly demeaned and undermined in front of your colleagues and are told to stay in your own lane. When you're given more attention for your contributions from your executive, you notice the relational aggression increases.

What's going on here?

Is this a realistic office scenario for a modern workplace?

Ask any woman in the workforce today, and she'll likely raise an eyebrow and nod her head sadly. This is *"mean girl"* behavior, and it's not just for junior high girls—it's everywhere from the playground to the board room.

And it's got to stop.

In this book, we'll learn what *mean girl* behavior is, how to survive it, and how to stop dishing it out. We'll learn powerful tools to come together as women, and how to wholeheartedly raise each other up in love and camaraderie. This world is big enough for all of us to be successful and when we learn to come together as women, we can become more powerful than we could have ever become on our own.

CRABS, CO-WORKERS, AND COMPETITION

Some tell the story that when fisherman catch crabs, they've learned they don't even need to keep a lid on the crab pot. You see, if one crab starts to crawl up to the top of the crab pot, another crab quickly comes along and pulls it back down right next to the other crabs. The crabs control the other crabs and make sure that not one crab gets out of the crab pot.

It's the same way for us. We're working hard, improving ourselves, growing and striving, trying to climb up from the bottom of the crab pot to get to that next level, but every time we do, another crab comes along and pulls us back down.

How often do you see your coworkers *and especially women* fighting and competing with each other and pulling each other down?

That's exactly what mean girl behavior is.

- A feeling of competition instead of a spirit of camaraderie

- Sabotaging others in order to improve our own situation. Bullying in an attempt to shore up our feelings of insecurity

- Hurting others in a mistaken attempt to make ourselves look better in comparison

- Fearing that another's success means that we are somehow less

HERE'S JANICE'S STORY
(names have been changed)

I moved into a new department about three years ago. At the beginning of my new position, my co-worker (I'll call her Fran) was cordial, but as time went on, she began to show her true self. I'll never forget the first holiday season I was in the department. I suggested we do a Secret Santa. Fran quickly told me there was already a Secret Santa club in place for the group, and I'd have to find someone else to do it with. Even though I worked in the department, it was clear I wasn't invited to be a part of it. She even pulled everyone together, in front of me, to pick their Secret Santa names.

At lunch time, Fran collected everyone in the department to go to lunch and skipped me. All birthdays are celebrated, except for mine. Fran has weekend BBQ's to which I am not invited and on Monday everyone talks about how fun it was.

I've chosen not to drag my executive into this petty situation, but I must admit it hurts to not be included. At first, I felt hurt that the others in the department didn't stick up for me and ask why I wasn't invited, but I realized that Fran was bullying them as well.

I even watched in amazement as she successfully bullied my executive into changing a decision, he'd made with me.

I've dealt with mean girls and bullies before and I know I can't change them. I know I only have control over myself and can choose how I react and behave in her presence. Don't get me wrong, this does not help the hurt. But I have the knowledge that I have control over my own actions and reactions.

Knowing how her actions have made me feel, I try my very best to behave in a manner that is empowering to others and, in turn, empowers me.

Janice has learned an important lesson that we can't force others to change—all we can change is our own reactions. Victor Frankl famously stated this, after suffering at the hands of Nazi prison guards.

"Everything can be taken from a man but one thing: the last of human freedoms - to choose one's attitude in any given set of circumstances, to choose one's own way." (Man's Search for Meaning, Victor Frankl, 1946)

Being bullied in an office situation may not be as dramatic, but what can we do as women to help and build each other up, instead of tearing each other down—instead of pulling each other back into the crab pot? The answer may be as simple as two small things:

- An "inner circle" of supportive women

- A clear vision of your own great worth

I've been blessed in my life to have both of these things, forming a source of strength, conviction, and encouragement for me. I've come to the realization that they can work for you, too.

CHAPTER**TWO**

How My Inner Circle
Came To Life

"No one, absolutely no one, succeeds alone!
We all need each other to reach our highest potential."

One day, I was going through emails and I saw an out-of-the-blue opportunity. By the way, out-of-the-blue opportunities come to us because we're ready for the opportunity. This isn't a game of chance. It's a game of being ready when the opportunity appears. I read the email from Connie, who is the former Content and Conference Manager for a conference for which I've spoken since 2010. She shared that Kathy was looking for help with a special project and asked me to consult with her.

So, I gave it some thought. First of all, I only do this type of consult with those who I respect as a person and the work they do. Kathy has this in spades. A few years ago, I had the pleasure and privilege of seeing her speak and move the audience like a master.

Later that same day, I had the opportunity to have lunch with her and 10 attendees - AND she ended up sitting right next to me. It made a lasting impression on me to meet Kathy face-to-face and hear her words of wisdom while sitting next to her over lunch.

I didn't know at that moment how HUGE of an opportunity it would later become. Plus, here's the other thing—the whole reason why I got a seat at the table for lunch was because of my friend and former coworker, Debbie. She learned about the opportunity and shared it with me. It was an invitation only, private event. I wasn't invited. My name wasn't on the list. I simply tagged along with Debbie and asked Connie, who was manning the door, if there was room for me to join and she said, "Sure." You've always gotta ask!

> Things come to those who ask!
> And those who show up!

This was a perfect example of the two key things I talked about in Chapter One.

- A woman reached out with an opportunity to another woman (Inner Circle)

- I got brave and asked for the chance, because I have a clear vision of my worth

Two years after that amazing lunch, I received the email from Connie asking me to consider doing this special project with Kathy. This is what happens when you ask and show up. I don't believe it was coincidence.

At the time I got the email, I was preparing for a keynote I was to deliver in Silicon Valley for Executive Secretary LIVE. A woman by the name of Lucy Brazier is the CEO of this event and we met in 2015 on LinkedIn. Since that time frame, I've had the opportunity to speak at several of Lucy's conferences scattered around the world: Dubai, London, South Africa, Sydney and this year I'll be adding New Zealand to the list. Lucy is the type of woman who demonstrates what it means to lift other women up and to help them become the woman they were meant to be. I am part of this amazing group of women, this powerful inner circle of speakers scattered across the world and I credit this to Lucy.

Executive Secretary LIVE was the perfect opportunity to accomplish the work Kathy needed. At the conference, I was able to meet the right people and create the right connections to assist Kathy in just the right way.

Did you pick up on how many people were in my circle to make this opportunity happen? Debbie, Connie, Kathy, and Lucy. And, it took each of them pursuing her dream to weave us together. First, it took me pursuing my dream of becoming a professional speaker (I've got more about my inner circle supporting my dream in the next chapters). It took Lucy Brazier pursuing her dream of creating a platform for administrative assistants from around the world. It took Kathy pursuing her dream of becoming a professional speaker and powerhouse. Each person pursued her dream and those dreams wove us all together to do something powerful to create an incredibly powerful outcome. For me, it was an honor to work with Kathy and her team and play a part in the amazing work she's doing to help people move forward.

THE MAGIC OF BRAVELY ASKING

Here's the other mindboggling thing that happened. I decided to be courageous and ask. I sent the following email to Dave, the CFO of Kathy's business:

Dave, it has been a pleasure working with you and I would love to have the opportunity to do so again in the future. As you know, I'm also a professional speaker and I certainly aspire to reach Kathy's levels of success one day. I actually have the attached picture on my desk with a hand-written note from an accomplished speaker that reads, "Think Bigger!" I'm curious if you'd be willing to refer me for future speaking requests that Kathy can't fit into her schedule? I believe we both have a similar heart-centered approach to topics that speak widely to diverse audiences. If this feels right to you, we can talk about a referral fee that makes sense. I deeply believe we're connected to people for a reason. The chance of us working together is a miracle in itself. If I hadn't pursued my dream of becoming a professional speaker, I wouldn't have met Kathy at the conference a few years ago. I wouldn't have had the relationship with Connie who referred me to you. I wouldn't have had the opportunity to consult with and help Kathy. We're all just an ask and actions away from where we're supposed to be in this big beautiful world. All it takes is courage and connection to get there. My signature keynote is "Developing the Power of Your Inner Circle" and what we just experienced is definitely that type of powerful connection.

No matter what you choose, know that I am grateful for the opportunity to work with you and to be a small part of what you and Kathy are doing to help others. I have the utmost respect for your work and am proof that you are making a difference!

As soon as I sent the email, I started doubting myself. I reached out to a few friends and said things like, "OMG! I'm freaking out!" Thankfully, I have an incredible inner circle who talked me off the shelf of self-doubt and reassured me it was a business offering and I wasn't to doubt the possibilities.

Guess what the outcome was?
He said YES!

How often do we not ask? How often do we fill ourselves with self-doubt? All too often! The way to increase your courage and be bold enough to "ask" is to build an inner circle. That way you'll have the relationships to carry you when you feel weak, to lift you up to where you want to be, to push you forward and to shine the light on possibilities.

What's the big deal about having an inner circle? Why should you care? To make your dreams a reality – that's why! As cliché as this may sound, it's absolutely why! There's no way I would've become a professional speaker who has traveled across the United States and to Dubai, London, South Africa, Australia, New Zealand, Paris and Spain if I hadn't created my own inner circle.

Let me give you one huge reason why –
to make your goals a reality –
that's why!

I wanted to be a speaker and author from as far back as I can remember. I grew up next door to the grade school and every summer I would dumpster dive for teaching materials which I would take home and play teacher. I would teach anyone who would listen… most of the time it was my sisters or neighborhood kids, and sometimes, it was with my Barbies. When I started babysitting, I had a whole new audience.

My grade school best friend and I would write stories in spiral notebooks and pretend we were authors. It's no surprise that today we're both published authors.

When I saw my first professional speaker, I knew that was exactly what I wanted to do. There was no doubt in my mind. I remember sitting there in the audience and reaching out for my husband's hand. I had energy bubbling up inside of my body and tears streaming down my cheeks because the dream was so real. It was a feeling of knowing that is exactly what I'm supposed to do, what I've been called to do.

Here's the problem—you don't just announce to the world that you want to be a speaker and like magic the speaking engagements appear. I didn't know how to get started and I struggled to make it a reality.

I slowly started to get some speaking engagements, 1 or 2 conferences a year. I'd speak for local groups and occasionally, I would be asked to speak for an organization. I was struggling to get more opportunities. Then, one day, all of that changed, I was speaking for several conferences a year and for the top Fortune 500 companies, as well. On top of all that, I started speaking internationally! Can you imagine not ever being outside of the United States and then being asked to speak in Dubai?

Shortly after that, I was invited to speak in London, twice in one year, and then South Africa and Sydney, Australia. All of this happened because of building my inner circle.

I was ecstatic to become a professional international speaker! At first, my focus was all about me hitting that goal and about the opportunity to travel to amazing places. This was only the beginning of what I later realized.

What I discovered was that it was the people who I met that I hold closest to my heart. People like Lucy from London, Laura from Belgium, Lizzy from Paris, Eth from New Zealand, Diana from Germany, Teri from South Africa, Anel from Dubai—not to mention all the amazing people from the US, like Melba and Libby from NY, Collette from CA, and my mastermind sisters, Chrissy, Lisa and Julie. The list goes on and on.

My life has been forever changed. My inner circle has conversations about our dreams and goals. We share stories about our successes and ask for help to move past our failures. We're vulnerable with each other. There's no façade. We ask for advice and counsel AND WE TRUST EACH OTHER. There is no competition between us. We're not competing with each other, instead we're completing each other.

I found my tribe, my inner circle of people, scattered around the world. We have big dreams and goals and together we're changing the world. I invite you to join us.

We truly are in this together and the one thing I know for certain is, if you want to change the world, it takes a group of people going after the same cause and believing they can make a difference.

People in an inner circle know that we rise by lifting others. This is exactly what has happened because of building my inner circle.

We rise by lifting others

THE BEGINNINGS OF MY INNER CIRCLE

One of the people in my inner circle is Lucy. We met on LinkedIn about five years ago. Isn't it amazing the people you can meet over social media? I had never even heard of Lucy until seeing her post on LinkedIn.

It all began with a post she made about the value of partnerships. I made what I thought was an insignificant comment on her post. I simply told her that I appreciated her article and was aligned with her thinking. I had no idea what that comment would lead to.

At that time, Lucy was also building her business and her career as a publisher and a speaker and my comment meant a lot to her. Today *Executive Secretary* magazine has over 45,000 connections on LinkedIn but back then she didn't have that foundation. My comment meant a great deal to her. She was just getting started herself and clearly sought that kind of support.

I remember hearing her introduce me as inimitable (in –im – a – table) – first I had to look it up, because I had no idea what it meant. To my surprise, I learned inimitable means:

So good or unusual as to be impossible to copy; unique!

Wow! Talk about a confidence booster.

Are you familiar with the Pygmalion effect? It's a phenomenon where higher expectations lead to increased performance. This is exactly what happened for me because of Lucy. She treated me as if I had already become the speaker I wanted to be. Because of this, I make sure that each and every time I speak for her, I deliver. I never want to let her down.

This new level of confidence propels me forward and helps me believe my dreams are possible. I can achieve what my heart yearned for and whispered to me as a young 20- something woman.

What about you? What dreams and goals has your heart yearned for and whispered to you?

Remember, I met Lucy on LinkedIn and she's now part of my inner circle. It all started because of a seemingly insignificant comment on a post she made. One small comment. Think about that for a moment. One small comment on social media or face- to-face has the power of leading to a rich connection.

Without developing an inner circle, my dream of becoming an author and professional speaker wouldn't have ever happened. When I first started speaking, it was done under the safety net of co-presenting with my dear friend and co-worker, Darlene. We brainstormed, outlined and rehearsed together month-after-month to get ready for our first conference speaking opportunity. We believed in each other and shored each other up through our nerves, doubts and uncertainty. AND we celebrated after each win! We also had a healthy lesson learned session to evaluate how we did after each speaking engagement—we had so much to learn.

Celebrate your successes and falling short!
Each experience will build your strengths,
talent and character towards your journey to greatness.

Embrace the fact that you'll never be ready. Even if you do the work, you'll never feel 100% ready to step up front and do what's in your heart. You need to step forward, raise your hand and open your mouth anyway!

I can guarantee you, we never felt ready. We took months and months to prepare for each and every speaking engagement -- stayed up late, got up early and still didn't' feel ready. We prayed and practiced. We visualized. We spoke positive affirmations. We breathed confidence into each other AND still didn't feel ready. We had to make the leap! Once we did, we loved it and began the journey toward the dream.

Was it scary? YES! Was there a parachute to escape? NO! Did we fall short? YES! Did we succeed? YES! All these things were true.

I've never met a successful executive, artist, speaker, author, athlete or any successful person who said they were 100% ready and confident of success. You must step out and up anyway. This is part of the process of honing your craft of becoming what you've dreamed of becoming. It's the fire you need to go through to get where you want to go. A great coach, a great mentor will lead and guide you along the way, but you'll be the one doing the work and taking the chance to get to the end state of your goal.

I attended my first professional conference in 2003, the Administrative Professionals Conference (APC) in Florida at the Dolphin Hotel. It was truly life changing.

I had no idea what to expect or what was about to happen to me and my career. When I walked into that huge conference room and saw 2000 admins in one room, it blew my mind. I began dreaming. Dreaming of all that I wanted to accomplish. On my list was:

• Become a member of the APC Advisory Council

• Become a speaker for APC

• Become an Author

• Become the Emcee for APC

I'm here to tell you all of those dreams became a reality! It didn't happen overnight, it wasn't easy, and it didn't happen because I got a special invitation. It happened because I created my own opportunities by building relationships! First with the conference coordinator and those working the conference, next with the attendees. These relationships broadened my inner circle and helped to create more opportunities. I also spoke my dream into reality by telling my coworkers and friends and husband what I wanted to do. They become a huge part of my inner circle. A group of people who believed in me and encouraged me to go after my dream.

Here's how it happened:

In 2003, when I was attending for the first year, I was sitting in a break out session listening to Judi Moreo, author of "You Are More Than Enough" and as real as I was sitting there, my dream of becoming a professional speaker was re-planted. I turned to my friend and colleague, Debbie, and told her I wanted to be a speaker. Here's what was so amazing, she didn't laugh. She just said very distinctly – I don't!

I looked through the conference program and I saw there was an APC Advisory Council made up of administrative professionals from various industries and places in the world. I thought, "Wow! I want to be on the council." I talked with a few of the APC team including Lisa and others who were most helpful in pointing me in the right direction.

I got the opportunity to serve on the Council in 2009 and 2010. Serving on the Advisory Council was a rich opportunity to see the conference from all angles. One of the serendipities of serving on this council was the relationships I was able to create. In fact, Rocky and Stacy served on the council with me and we've continued to stay in touch with each other and are definitely part of my inner circle.

I became a speaker for APC in 2010 and I've now been a speaker for APC every year since.

In 2014, I became the author of *"NOT, Just an Admin!"* I had been speaking for a few years and hadn't published my own book. It was a huge dream of mine to become a published author. Up to this point, I had published a chapter *in "Life Choices, Putting the Pieces Together"* and had a few articles published in magazines. What I wanted was my own book.

I had been invited to speak at the International Association of Administrative Professionals Conference (IAAP) and was preparing for my upcoming conference presentation and thought, "I don't want to speak again and not have my own book." I had recently read, "Desire Map" by Danielle LaPorte and learned she wrote her book in three months! Guess how much time I had? You guessed it… three months.

I called Judi Moreo with Turning Point International publishing and here's what happened:

Me: "Besides working really hard, what do I have to do to have my book written, published and printed in three months?

Judi: "I need a chapter a week beginning this week!"

And that's exactly what I did. I got focused, I got busy, I got incredibly determined.

Before you think I had the luxury of taking a sabbatical to have this perfect environment of no interruptions and creativity space, think again! I was working full-time, preparing for my speaking engagement, a wife, mom, grandmother and living life during these three months as well. In fact, this was during the time that my grandson, Damon, was diagnosed with leukemia.

The entire time I was writing my book, he was at Children's Hospital or Ronald McDonald house. I was often writing while in the car traveling to Spokane, in the hallway of Children's Hospital or Ronald McDonald house late at night or early in the morning. The timing wasn't right. The environment wasn't great. I was tired, emotional, exhausted and scared. I didn't feel ready, but I did it anyway. In some ways, it was an emotional outlet, an escape from the pain of watching my son, daughter-in-law and grandson fight the cancer fight.

After a three-year journey, we were incredibly blessed to have completed the cancer treatment journey and today have a healthy seven-year-old little boy who is handsome, filled with energy, and as bright as you can possibly imagine. What a blessing.

The fire of this journey provided strength and increased our faith and belief that:

There's always something to be thankful for.

My daughter put a sticky note on my back that read: "Do not disturb: Author in progress!!" Having her at home observing me write was an incredible blessing as well. She was going through her own journey of going to college at WSU and had her own set of challenges. Seeing her mom go after her dream, even after turning 50, let her know that dreams are possible at any age.

After three months, my book was completed, published and printed. I remember talking with Judi and learning the proof was ready. I was so proud of this accomplishment. When the first box of books was delivered to my house, I couldn't wait to open the box to see, touch, and smell the book. The goal was accomplished! The books arrived on time and sold out at the conference!

Without Judi, my dear husband, Renè, and many friends and family, accomplishing this dream of becoming an author would not have been possible. I needed each person who played a role in that journey. Talk about the power of an inner circle! I am incredibly grateful and thankful to all!

> "Your world can be completely different based on the people you meet, and that you allow to influence you."

In 2017, I became the emcee at APC. This was another huge goal. I had seen several amazing emcees over the years and like the other situations, I told my friends I wanted to do that as well. I let APC know I was interested and, after much hard work of building connections and my reputation, that dream was accomplished.

My question for you is,

What do you want?

What is your dream?

The way you're going to get there is through hard work, which means you've got to hustle even when you're tired and when it's not convenient. Most of all you've got to hustle when you aren't feeling confident. Your kryptonite, your strength lies in building an inner circle. Your inner circle will encourage you to move past the times when you're filled with self-doubt, when you don't have the strength, they'll be the ones that lift you up and inspire you to move forward. Never doubt the power of believing in yourself <u>before</u> you become the woman you were meant to be.

CHAPTER**THREE**

The Process of Discovery

Years ago, when I was in high school, I was in DECA. It was a program that prepared young people for the business world and through that program I got a position as a part time secretary for a furniture company. This was long before computers, or even the modern "Selectric" typewriter. I typed on a manual typewriter! I worked with carbon paper in triplicate, had colored white-out - one for each of the colors of the carbon copies. Thank God for advanced technology!

I had been working there for a few months, when my DECA teacher asked to meet with me after class. I sat across his desk and he asked me, "How is your job going?" I told him it was going great. He then pushed a file folder towards me and asked, "Is this your work?"

I opened the file folder and to my embarrassment the letter I saw was the perfect example of what not to do. It was filled with mistakes and white out so thick that it had cracked. There were grammar and typo mistakes and it was messy and sloppy. The old typewriters had ink ribbons and when you were correcting a mistake with white out, you often touched the ribbon. When you took the letter out of the typewriter, your fingerprints would leave an imprint on the letter.

There's not a manager or business owner out there who would want to sign a letter like that. It represents them and their company. I quickly turned to the next letter hoping it was better, but to my embarrassment each letter was the same.

When my teacher asked me, "Is this your work?" I wanted to say, "NO" but the problem was... my initials were at the bottom of the letters. I was humiliated.

Holding back tears, I said "Yes. This is my work."

He then asked me the most impressionable question I've ever been asked:

"Is this what you want your reputation to be?"

When I heard that question, my heart sank. Tears streamed down my cheeks as I said, "I don't want to be considered a failure or a poor performer!" I don't remember anything else my teacher said. All I felt then and know now was he believed in me. He was kind, didn't berate me, and didn't make me feel small. Instead, he wanted to help me. He showed he cared about me enough to talk my employer into letting me keep my job, to give me a second chance so I could prove I could do better. My employer agreed, and I had the opportunity to prove my abilities and reshape my reputation.

That moment of feedback, mentoring and compassion was life changing. The reputation and mentoring pieces to this story are profound, but there's one more critical detail in the story. He approached the conversation with a simple question "How is your job going?"

My DECA teacher took the time to create a second chance for me. What he did by asking that very simple question was he engaged in a process of discovery. That process created connection, trust and an earnest desire to do well.

Asking questions and being interested in others is key to creating your inner circle.

"You can make more friends in two months
by becoming interested in other people
than you can in two years by trying to get
people interested in you."
~ Dale Carnegie

My husband, Renè, is absolutely brilliant at this. Here's what's interesting. He gets complimented all the time for being a great conversationalist. He always laughs and says he's just really good at asking questions and listening.

Think about the last networking event you attended. What did you talk about? If you talked about the weather, or some other type of small talk and didn't move past that, were you really creating a connection?

Think about a time where the person you were talking to was more interested in passing out his business card than creating a true connection with you. Or, the person who kept looking past you after asking you a question, indicating that he was just filling up time until someone more important arrived. What about the time you met up with someone and the talking was all one-sided or when the person waxed on and on about what he's been doing and how great his life has been going?

These types of conversations and interactions don't work, because they lack connection. It's these types of interactions that give us anxiety when we hear the word "Networking."

We've all had more than our fair share of these surfacey, plastic interactions. Yet, we often do this. It's our default setting to start talking about the weather or something trivial.

If this is what we usually do, what should we do instead?

You might remember that my DECA teacher didn't start by giving me feedback on my letter. He asked me about my reputation which was a valuable interaction and it stayed with me to this day. But remember, he started with, "How's your job going?"

He didn't lay into me and start lecturing me. He did a very important and powerful thing. He went through an act of discovery. An act of discovery with me. Most of us rush into something by telling people how it's from our perspective and show no curiosity about the other person.

> How do you create an inner circle?
> Through the act of discovery.

At the time of writing this book, I'm still working full time as the Chief Executive Assistant at Pacific Northwest National Laboratory. During my tenure, I've worked for three different Laboratory Directors, which is equivalent to the President of an organization. The last two Lab Directors were Steve and Mike.

Mike and Steve couldn't be more different. They are complete opposites in almost every single way. If I interacted with Steve the same way I did Mike, it wouldn't be effective because they are completely different people. For example, when Mike would come into the office on Monday morning, he'd walk in and say, "Good Morning. How are you? How was your weekend?" which was code for, get your cup of coffee, come in and let's chat about the weekend. Then, we'd talk about business. On the other hand, Steve would walk into the office on Monday morning and say, "Good Morning. How are you? How was your weekend?" I responded with, "Good Morning. I'm doing great. How are you?" Steve would go into his office and focus immediately on work. Later we'd meet to talk about business, and at the end of the day, we may or may not talk about our weekend. I had a great relationship with both of these executives, because I took the time to actively discover the interests of each of these men well enough to know what their goals were and how to help them be successful.

This is the same way it works for creating a connection with other people and creating your inner circle.

CHAPTER**FOUR**

How to Create an
Inner Circle

Developing an inner circle is a lot like finding your true love… you must allow yourself to be vulnerable, open and let your guard down. You must take the risk to get the reward.

Risks like:

- having the courage to walk up to someone and say hello.

- taking the time to discover someone and see if you can create a connection, build rapport and learn if and how you can help each other.

- putting yourself out there on social media, all for the purpose of building connections.

Here's what we do to try to meet people. We white-knuckle our way through one networking event after another, hoping to make a connection. The problem is we haven't been taught how to connect. We've been taught how to network. In fact, often when people RSVP for an event, they don't show up because of fear—fear they won't fit in, fear they aren't good enough, or fear they won't know what to say to someone else. These fears are so great they'd rather miss out than take a chance of being rejected, yet again.

When we're experiencing fear, we shut down, close up and armor up. We build a wall so thick no one can get in… we won't let people in to see our hearts and our visions. We hide our emotions and we mentally shut down. When you put up a wall, close down, and hide – you can't connect.

The reason we have these fears and this anxiety all stems from one single cause.

These problems take place because we lack connection. A lot of people talk about connection, but they often lack the critical ingredient for making it happen.

The way to move past fear is through action. The way you create an inner circle is by going through the act of discovery with another person. Here's a model to help you.

Consciously, carefully, thoughtfully choose each person in your inner circle. You'll become like the five people you spend the most time with, so choose your inner circle wisely.

Ask yourself these questions:

1. Who is influencing you?

- Are you mindful of their influence on your life?

- Are your closest friends, family and colleagues affecting you positively or negatively?

2. Who are you emulating?

- Are you doing the same thing over and over and hoping for different results and a better life?

3. Are you modeling behaviors that would attract meaningful connection?

• In other words, would you want to connect with you?

We aren't separated by our personal life and work life. We are one person. Think about that when creating your inner circle. Consider all the areas of your life, not just your career, and ask yourself, who is pulling you forward? When you're looking for your inner circle find people who have more knowledge and experience than you.

Write down names of people for each area of your life.

People who...

1. you respect and admire.

2. are where you want to be.

3. you would contact in the middle of a challenge.

4. will lift you up and encourage you.

5. will tell you what you need to hear even if it hurts a little.

6. believe in you and your dreams.

7. will propel you forward towards your dreams and goals.

8. you discover by saying hello, going through an act of discovery and finding out how you can help each other.

The more you focus on being your authentic self, the more the right people will be attracted to you. You don't just need people who like you, you need people to lead you towards your purpose in life.

We become the average
of the five people
we spend the most time with.
Choose carefully.

**Write the names of the people you admire, under
each category below.**

Health: What do you want for yourself in your
health, fitness or self-care? Who do you know that
is the epitome of health? Who do you go to with your
questions about health? Who has this area of their life
really dialed in and would be willing to teach you?

All too often this area of our lives is put on hold,
especially for women. And yet, we all know we can't
pursue our mission in life if we aren't healthy. We
can't help others if we aren't whole. This is why it's so
important to surround yourself with people who can
help you.

Career: What do you want in terms of your career
or in your business? Do you want to launch a new
product or expand your team? Do you want to freshen
up your resume or ask for a raise? Do you want to
write a book? Do you want to create more authentic
connections? Who do you know who has a successful
career or business and could help you?

Lifestyle: This is all about how you like to spend your
time when you aren't doing your work. This could be
about play, travel, arts, expression, dance, or music.
This can also be about creating a lifestyle that makes
you feel happy and complete, instead of a lifestyle
filled with stress and heaviness. You get to decide
what lifestyle means to you. Who has a lifestyle you
admire and could help you?

Relationships: Think about the most important people in your life. Who are they? What do you want those relationships to look like, feel like, be like? What do you want to experience with these people that you love? What are some improvements you can make in your relationships that are going to require some attention and focus and who is going to help you make that happen? Who do you know that has successful relationships? Who are your role model parents, grandparents, uncles or aunts? Who do you know that's married, obviously in love, demonstrates respect and still enjoy each other's company? Who is an amazing friend who could help you become a better friend?

Spirit: Have you met someone who seemed to shine or glow? Someone who radiated with joy? This is the type of person who has figured out how to feed her spirit. This can be about religion, meditation, service to others or none of the above. It's up to you to decide what spirit means to you. What's important is that you're feeding your soul and because of that, you're at peace within yourself and radiate joy. Who do you know that fits this picture and can help you?

Wealth: This is about financial security instead of living a life based on fear and financial worries. Security means different things to different people. Focus on what a healthy financial picture means to you. For some, it might mean a large sum of money in the bank. For others, it may be about retirement. You want to feel confident when it comes to your financial standing. Who has this figured out and can help you?

As you go through this exercise, avoid the urge to censor yourself. Avoid the self-doubt of thinking no one would be willing to help you because they're too busy; or you aren't good enough or important enough for someone else to take time to help you. Simply write down the names of people who you admire. I'll help you with the self-doubt in a future chapter.

Every single person you meet on this planet can teach you something, if you're open to it. Your life can be completely different based on the people you meet and allow to influence you. Open yourself up to the people around you!

We all need mentors and coaches to help us move forward. I've hired several coaches in my career and I guarantee you I would not be writing this book if I hadn't taken that step and made the investment. Remember, "No one, absolutely no one, succeeds alone."

Surround yourself with people
who lift you up!

Read this story and consider how you may have handled the situation. If this woman came to you for advice what would you tell her?

ANONYMOUS STORY – MEAN GIRLS AND MY DREAM JOB!

My career dream was to be an executive assistant (EA) working in the top levels of a company where I could showcase my skills. Having evolved from being a receptionist to personal assistant (PA)/ Secretary to an EA with the aptitude and qualities of a business assistant, I was excited about the new role providing genuine right-hand support to an executive with such a huge role and responsibility I was more familiar with working in small sized companies but felt I wanted to do more, add value and be part of a larger organization.

*****

The company was a large corporation, with offices in an iconic skyscraper with panoramic views of London and beyond particularly on a clear sunny day. The open floor plans were vast with rows of uniformly sparse workstations with executives' offices around the exterior walls. Personal assistants were seated among their respective teams; I couldn't differentiate them from any other colleague, initially.

*****

"Good morning...Hello, how are you doing?" from random colleagues in corridors and in the kitchen/ coffee area, smiley introductions and get-to-know-you conversations took place. "It's such a great place to work, everyone gets on and helps each other out" - was the recurring theme. "If you need any help, just ask, there are no egos here, everyone will go out of their way to help, I promise". Human Resources arranged an Assistants lunch at a local restaurant. The team laughed, moaned, enjoyed good food, moaned, interrogated me on personal life and career to date. I noticed raised eyebrows, rolling eyes, sentences cut-off in mid flow, competitive redirection and comments on my wearing a suit which when challenged, were brushed off as innocent banter. The hour drew to a close, my focus was returning to the office and my executive's intense schedule to get under control.

*****

The schedule was a nightmare consisting of non-existent to basic information with no detail of future board /committee / client meetings my executive was scheduled to attend. Meeting with Chairman/CEOs EA who 'managed' the schedule previously proved fruitless - every time I went to her desk, she was either on Facebook or online shopping. My request for onboarding, training and to review everything on the schedule, board and committee obligations and responsibility, future travel plans, internal/external events fell on deaf ears. Frustration built as I regularly called her, visited her desk, emailed, instant messaged and was outright ignored. How can I function without the background, the papers, the tickets and confirmation emails? My performance was suffering - snide comments made about my "not coping" that I need to give it time and not be too hard on myself! Offers of help came from other PAs but not the help I needed - I just needed my inquiries answered about the company systems and processes, not how to color code Outlook! No one responded to specific questions and I couldn't believe a PA would leave another PA to prevent me or my boss from doing our jobs. Approaching other PA's for help resulted in silence or insincere ignorance. It was clear, this was a collective failing, it was the culture of the company, egotistical, self-serving, incommunicative, built on covering one's own behind!

*****

Clearly ostracized, walking along corridors or anywhere in the building now meant no social engagement except for Oscar winning performances when senior partners were present. Conversations with other non-PA colleagues in the kitchen or coffee area, would be interrupted abruptly and hijacked. The Chairman/ CEOs EA, as the leader of the clique had a "sidekick" - they both had worked at the company for years, spoke condescendingly and created unnecessary barriers. Once there was a formal dinner and, shamelessly, the group of PA's were nearby discussing their plans for meeting up and attending the dinner together

*excluding me from any of the discussion. I saw the
embarrassment in the faces of some of the "entourage"
but to me they were equally guilty. I decided to protect
myself and my executive as best as I could, but the
realization hit and hit hard, this nightmare scenario, my
dream job was in a toxic environment with no visible
prospects of the situation improving. It was widespread
problem with the PA's across all departments, I was left
out in the cold and will always be.*

*****

*"How are you getting on?" people would ask with
excitement and an expectant smile. Lying became
second nature; hiding the truth was taking its toll. On
a daily basis, pertinent information wasn't shared,
but they would claim it was given, collaboration on
business projects did not happen but they would claim
they offered to walk me through. Emails were not
responded to, but they would claim I had been told.
Reprimanded for failure to deliver, I tried explaining
the situation without coming across as a victim - he
recruited me for my resilience - he had pressure of
his own to deal with. The disbelief that a team of PA's
had affected mine and my executives' performance,
business and reputation was hard to swallow - I saw
no future there but saw no way out either.*

*****

*Work had become a battlefield in an unnecessary war
with supposedly mature women, who were wives and
mothers, going out of their way to "win at all costs".
Taking a few deep breaths and playing loud music
through my iPhone headset, I entered that tower every
morning affirming to "..be positive, be brave, be the
person you were before entering that lion's den". I
knew my day would be wasted double checking every
detail received from the PA team in case I was being*

set up to fail. My time wasted providing explanatory responses to my boss, in my defense, when the EA highlighted an error or omission of mine - it was wasted time, effort and energy. Disappointed, exhausted, disheartened, being an EA was my chosen career path, this was my dream role in a midsize company in a picturesque location with panoramic views and prospects for future advancement and opportunities. Where do I go? What do I do? Health is worth more than this, isn't it? Can I risk losing everything, falling behind with mortgage, bills? Is it worth it?

*****

I am worth it and now happier, healthier and healing from these experiences (and much more). I am unemployed despite best efforts to the contrary with the added problem having to explain why I left my last role. I know walking away was the best decision I made in the circumstances. Life is too short, and it's a big world out there!

Imagine for a moment how different this story would have ended if she had a powerful inner circle. She could have been given tools to handle the women she worked with; she could have had a supportive group to help her get through this toxic environment. AND an inner circle may have helped her get to the same outcome feeling more whole and more prepared to look for a new position. In fact, I bet she would have had several leads and possibly a new job before she quit this nightmare job!

We each have our circle of influence and due to technology and social media, we're more connected than ever. When you find yourself in a work environment that is toxic and filled with sabotage, with no end in sight, it's time to reach out to your inner circle for support. Let them know that you're interested in new opportunities, you'll be surprised at the readily available information they have and will willingly share with you to help you move forward – towards your next "dream job!"

CHAPTER**FIVE**

What holds you back?

THE VISION OF YOUR LIFE

Years ago, I had the pleasure of hearing Martha Beck, Oprah's life coach, deliver a keynote at a conference. She was absolutely spellbinding. Towards the end of the day, I was sitting with my friend, Darlene, in one of the conference hotel restaurants. We noticed Martha walking by, passing the restaurant and heading to the pool. The odd thing was she was fully dressed, shoes and all, and pulling her suitcase. We had a brave thought. She's looking for somewhere to go and why not capitalize on the moment and invite her to join us? AND she did. She ordered a strawberry milkshake with whipped cream and as she enjoyed her milkshake, we enjoyed the conversation, soaking up her wisdom as she gently coached us.

Martha is one of the smartest and most grounded people I've ever met. Martha shared that she believes we've been set up for a lifetime of comparison and competition literally from our first breath. When we were born, a doctor probably assigned us an Apgar score, a number indicating how our muscle tone and heart rate scored. Throughout toddlerhood, the assessments continued as our height and weight were constantly compared with our peers. And then, along came school. With every test, report card, and athletic event, we got another ranking. Eventually, we joined the working world, competing for jobs and striving to outperform colleagues so we'd get the promotion.

She essentially witnessed to us that we were Shaman, that we were both wearing the shaman sign, that we had work to do and would one day be in Africa helping people.

Darlene and I were both excited and a little afraid of what was to come. Sometimes that happens when someone has such conviction about you, especially when you haven't thought of yourself that way or had that vision for your life. (I'll tell you later about my trip to South Africa! Yes, just like Martha said, it happened!)

PLAY TO WIN

I grew up with two sisters. My dad made sure we could hold our own whether on a basketball court, baseball field or at the card table. Often, when playing cards, my sisters and I would start laughing and talking and dad would quickly put us in check by asking, "Are we playing cards or talking?" That meant "get serious and play to win!"

It was the same in sports. We all played basketball, softball and volleyball. My competitiveness and "play to win" spirit drove me to practice more than just during the arranged practices. I practiced shooting baskets across the street at the grade school and scrimmaged at the church gym…often playing with the boys to help increase my talent and up my game. I wasn't ever an all-star player, but I learned how to make my small size work for me by becoming a pretty good ball handler and sinking most of my foul shots, plus 3 point shots.

During tryouts for the high school team, I was matched up to scrimmage against one of the best players. I remember feeling incredibly nervous, and then suddenly, I was driving past her to the basket. Instead of continuing towards the basket to make the shot, I hesitated. I stopped myself because in my mind she was better than me and because of this mindset, I didn't think there was any chance I could get past her and score. She noticed my hesitation and said, "Go! Don't stop!" Her comment pushed me forward.

Can you imagine what would happen
if this is what most women said to each other?

She didn't seize the moment to crucify me with a confident, "Who do you think you are?" comment. Instead, she used her confidence to propel me forward.

THE COMPARISON TRAP

When you consider the typical life experiences of competition, comparison and judgment, it's no wonder that in our day-to-day lives, and especially in the workplace, we tend to be guarded. We carry past baggage of being hurt. We're too afraid to be open and vulnerable with each other. We get stuck in the comparison trap and game of competition. Which leads to the "I'm not good enough" dead-end.

We look at another woman and without even hesitating, our subconscious minds plant questions in our heads...questions like:

- Is she smarter than me?

- Is she prettier than me?

- Is she more successful than me?

- Does she have a higher education?

- Does she live in a nicer home?

- Is she married to a better husband?

- Are her children more successful than my children?

- Is she a better mother than me?

These questions, and so many more, swirl around and around in our minds.

How often does this negative programming hold you back? You can get so engulfed with perfectionism and comparison that you allow your brilliance, creativity and spark to vanish. It's easy to get caught in the comparison trap when you look at a person you admire. You look at people who you think are so amazingly successful and think they have figured everything out and are crises free.

> "Why do we overestimate others
> and constantly question ourselves?"
> Enise Lauterbach

Stop telling yourself that other women and men you admire are perfect. The truth is we all have our own unique issues and challenges. The truth is no one is perfect.

The truth is we're each perfectly, imperfect human beings put on this earth for a reason—one of which is to celebrate each other. Let's come together as women and start lifting each other up and encouraging each other.

> "If you judge people,
> you have no time
> to love them."
> ~ Mother Teresa

Along with comparison, competition and feeling not good enough comes judgement.

As much as we hate to admit it, we all judge each other. We know it's not right, yet, it happens. In fact, we judge each other in seven short seconds and make eleven major decisions about each other! We size up what someone's education level is, their financial status, if they're trustworthy, competent, aggression, likeable, confident and if they have status or authority, their sense of humor and level of intensity. Sometimes our judgment stems from self-perseveration—we're naturally wired to survive—but most of the time, it's not. Instead, it's simply a habit and we do it without even thinking about it.

Social media has increased the amount of time we compare, judge and compete with each other. We spend much time and energy checking out what our friends, peers and colleagues are doing on Facebook, Instagram, LinkedIn, Snapchat and Pinterest.

"There's nothing that kills you in a race more
than looking over your shoulder and checking the lanes."
~ Brene Brown

We compare ourselves to what others post on social media even though we know that people are posting their best days and their best moments. We know this is the case and still we compare ourselves to these social media updates. We judge ourselves from behind the social media curtain.

You have the power to change this competition, comparison and judgment mindset. You don't have to settle for the status quo. You don't have to get sucked into negative *mean girl* behavior. You don't have to listen to the limiting beliefs you've been telling yourself. Limiting beliefs are negative stories you tell yourself, stories like "I'm not good enough. I'm not smart enough. I'm too old. I'm too young. I'll never get ahead." Instead of filling your mind with these doubts and uncertainties, you need to switch the channel and start telling yourself positive stories. Start saying, "I'm brilliant! I'm strong! I'm fully capable of achieving what I want in this world!" Fill your mind with positive possibilities. All it takes is deliberate thinking and action. What would happen if you changed your mindset? Are you open to the possibilities?

You can be the woman who:

- creates change in your workplace.

- invites others to join you.

- celebrates other women.

- builds an in inner circle for the purposes of lifting each other up!

I invite you to be that woman! Let's begin celebrating each other to create a brighter, better world for ourselves and our daughters.

I choose to surround myself
with phenomenal women
who are confident and secure enough
to know
there is enough room
for all of us
to make it to the finish line.

CHAPTER**SIX**

Mean Girl Behavior—
How to Survive It and
How to Stop Dishing
it Out

MEAN GIRLS THEN AND NOW

If you think back to middle school and high school days, you can likely remember a time when you had to deal with some level of *mean girl* behavior. Sadly, *mean girl* behavior doesn't end in grade school. I've seen this same behavior play out in the board room as much as I remember it in the class room. It can be so deceptive that the behavior isn't always noticed by everyone in the same room. However, if you pay attention, you'll notice the tone doesn't match the smile.

Typical *mean girl* behavior includes bullying, gossiping, and sabotaging, all done with intention to intimidate, undermine or degrade.

Mean girl behavior is also about belonging to an exclusive group and if you aren't in the group, you're ostracized. You're either "in" or you're "out". Sadly, women can be cruel to each other, including mocking or overly critiquing to the point of pettiness and exaggeration. Worse, we sometimes bond to another person over this cruel behavior because of our fear of being the one who is outcast from the group. We learn how to behave to fit in and go along with the pack either by joining in on the verbal attacks or by remaining a silent bystander.

When I first started writing this book, my plan was to have the focus be only on developing an inner circle.

As I began to write about what gets in the way, it became abundantly clear that I needed to address the problem of why more of us don't have an inner circle. I started hearing from women in my network about what gets in the way. Over and over again, it was *mean girl* behavior and the fear of that past behavior. I asked my network if they would share their stories to help other women learn how to navigate this negative behavior and to inspire us to change any negative behaviors we may be demonstrating.

Here's a story that showcases a typical *mean girl* office experience.

EDWINA LEE, FROM WHO'S THE REAL BOSS?

In my experience, if there's one type of mean girl (or guy!) you need to look out for, it's the one who seems to be 'in the pocket' of the boss. Strategically, this mean girl will do whatever is necessary to align herself alongside the boss as a source of protection when she finds her antics have landed her on the end of complaints to management and HR. And lucky for her, with that shield of protection, in the eyes of the boss, she can do no wrong.

I was witness to this type of mean girl in one organization, where a mean girl manager considered herself to be the 'second in charge' by her strategic alignment alongside the boss. She did everything in her power to bully and harass every member of the team attempting to pull rank and show her level of power over others. It became obvious to me that I was dealing with a mean girl on one of my first interactions with this manager when she introduced me to a new member of the team, saying "This is Edwina, she's the executive assistant to Mr. X, so her role is basically just doing whatever Mr. X asks her to!" Fully aware of my efforts in the industry to re-value the position of the executive assistant/personal assistant and move past the submissive stereotypes, she made this remark fully knowing it would get a rise out of me. More to the point though, she was adamant from the get-go to position herself as being more senior than me, and to demonstrate she was closer to our boss than I would ever be. Unfortunately, the mean girl streak did not end there, and it wasn't just me that was on the receiving end of it. From tracking the whereabouts (and toilet breaks!) of the entire team to getting close to individuals so they'd divulge sensitive personal information on themselves and others to her and constant social media stalking - she would then bring all the pieces of information she'd received on others to the boss to use it against them to help free them up, get them "unstuck" and move them out of the company. So why did she do this? And why would she want to terrorize her entire team and essentially be left with no one who wanted to work with her? Well, it was nothing more than a demonstration of power by a power-hungry individual, trying to claw her way higher and higher, no matter who she had to stomp on to get there. A young manager by any standards, she had worked her way through the company from a very young age with no formal education or formal business training. With only a long tenure in the one company under her belt, it was a high risk for her to ever try and get another job on the outside. So, anyone who seemed to be a threat to her personally and professionally within this organization was going to be sabotaged in true mean girl fashion.

To me though, this behavior was beyond just being a mean girl, but rather being a fully-fledged bully, which appeared to be tolerated by management and wasn't only detrimental to those on the receiving end, but also to the department and company. At any opportunity, this mean girl manager was in the boss's office painting the hideous pictures of others and sharing her thoughts on how to performance manage them 'out', and all the while promoting herself as being the angelic, wholesome and good employee delivering on this information responsibly.

My first piece of advice to others who find themselves on the end of these behaviors is to try and ignore the individual without adding fuel to the fire. Never display any sort of reaction to mean girls, no matter what they do to you. Displays of emotion, rage, or even hurt, will give them the power they're looking for, and ultimately the information on you that will then be used against you, such as you 'broke down' in the middle of the office, or you had a 'freak out' and started yelling out of nowhere. They will use your reactions to their advantage, so give them nothing and always remain calm and professional. Whilst emotional intelligence and a thick skin will go a long way in helping to deal with these types, even the most resilient can be brought down by their attacks, and whilst we can't control how others behave, we can choose how we behave and as such we should try and set an example for the better. Keep your own behavior at a level you can be proud of and that represents your own brand and reputation. Remember also, keep your commentary on these bully's contained, and don't allow further gossip to stem from your frustrations. It's difficult to contain your emotions and frustrations when you're on the receiving end of this sort of behavior, but only entrust a confidant to confide in outside of the workplace. Speaking to those in the workplace (other than HR and management) will only fuel the situation and contribute to subsequent attacks.

*****

The second course of action against these bullies is to stand up for yourself, or others, and challenge them in their disrespect. Set a standard of what is acceptable and what isn't. Be prepared to call them out when that line is crossed. You don't have to be confrontational or rude, but a quiet remark or a tap on the shoulder is well within your rights. If you don't have the courage to raise concerns with the way you're treated, then seek the support and advice from HR or management. Document the events that have happened and collate any relevant evidence to support your case. You want to avoid accusations and criticism when taking issues like this above, so focus instead on the behaviors, events and consequences for yourself and those around you. It can be difficult to reveal a mean girl, especially one who has put steps in place to protect themselves by siding with the boss. But, if you work in numbers, you can sometimes reveal what's really been going on and expose them for the mean girls they are.

Mean girl antics and bullying should never be tolerated, and if your prior efforts to ignore them, call them out and escalate the events to HR, don't have any penetration, then you're well within your rights to pack up your desk and leave. Leaving an organization for reasons of a bullying culture is accepted and respected, so don't ever believe that not tolerating these behaviors is a sign of weakness. Quite the opposite, in fact. And, don't ever think you're giving power to the bully by leaving. If a situation has become so serious that it's impacting your mental health, then that needs to be the priority. When you spend nearly half your waking week in the workplace, you need to ensure you're not in a toxic environment, so don't be afraid to take whatever steps are necessary to protect your workplace utopia.

HOW TO HANDLE *MEAN GIRL* BEHAVIOR:

If you come across *mean girl* behavior, first and foremost, this isn't about you and this isn't your fault. This is about that person's insecurities and comfort zones. Chances are she's suffering from the same feelings of fear, anger and lack of confidence that she fosters in others. Your best line of defense is to be:

- Confident: Avoid looking nervous or insecure. *Mean girls* are looking for weakness to exploit. Do your best to ignore them.

- Professional: Remain professional, no matter what a *mean girl* says or does, do not react as they'll use your reactions to their advantage. If you can't, then walk away.

- Seek out a mentor: Entrust a confidant to confide in and that can give you advice so that you'll be ready the next time. Learn how to stand up for yourself and set a standard of what is and what isn't acceptable.

- Authentic: Stay true to who you are, don't morph into a *mean girl* yourself in order to be accepted by a *mean girl.* Stand up for yourself.

And remember, leaving an organization for reasons of toxic *mean girl* culture is accepted and respected. Don't ever believe that not tolerating these behaviors is a sign of weakness.

Be Honest With Yourself About Your Own Actions (I'm guilty of being a *mean girl*, too.)

I'm sharing from experience that if you practice these behaviors, you'll spare yourself, and probably others, a great deal of heartache.

I'm ashamed to admit I've demonstrated *mean girl* behavior, too, even as an adult. I remember belonging to a powerful group of women. We came together quickly and were openly sharing our thoughts and dreams with each other. Some even felt safe enough to share past experiences with which they were still struggling. Together, we created a fair amount of transparency and vulnerability with each other.

Except for one. There was one woman in the group who wasn't as vulnerable and self-disclosing. She wasn't as connected to the rest of the group as others and the relationship wasn't as strong. Sadly, some of the group started to take on these negative *mean girl* behaviors to outcast her from the group. Looking back, I don't know why I went along with it. What drove me to act as a child? Why did I revert back to these outdated behaviors and tendencies?

I know now it happened because I didn't see it coming. I wasn't self-aware. I wasn't strong enough. I let fear get in the way.

• Fear of someone not being like the rest of us and causing us to be uncomfortable.

• Fear of not being accepted by the one person who was saying the woman didn't belong with the rest of us and listening to her instead of listening to my own heart and head.

I still feel horrible. It hurts my heart because now some of the relationships that were once beautiful barely exist. This is what the end state looks like when we behave like a *mean girl* – ultimately, it hurts everyone involved.

My friend, Wendy, shares her story which really hits home on this behavior.

WENDY VANARSDALE STORY

I believe the real value in what I have to share isn't in telling about the individual incidents of where I was a mean girl, or experienced mean girl behavior, mainly because I think we all have the same stories and there would be no real enlightenment in me sharing mine. The value I have to give is to share my journey of how I was able leave that behind.

At the heart of this behavior, I believe, lies a deep-rooted fear of not being "in the pack". For me, this started very early in life as I was raised in a religious sect that would honestly be classified as a cult. This religion taught that Armageddon was going to happen at any time and to survive you must be one of the accepted and embraced members of the religious sect. This isn't an excuse for my behavior. Giving an excuse is giving away your power to that excuse. I own my actions, but I share it as it helps to lay the foundation of why I was susceptible to this fear of not being "in the pack".

At the age of 20, I was excommunicated from "the pack" and left the religious sect. While at the time this was the toughest and scariest time in my life, I now recognize it as the biggest gift I was ever given. I was forced to pick up the pieces and rebuild my life with an entirely new pack - and through this I learned two very important foundational lessons that have blessed me.

First: Take back your power

When you base your own self-worth on the opinion of others, you're essentially giving them your pen and letting them to write your story. In this state, you'll always be at the mercy of others for your happiness. Take back that pen! You set your value, and the *moment you realize this you'll be on the path to a much happier life. I learned through my experience that I was in charge of my life, nobody else, and **I could choose my "pack"**. That was the big lesson for me – I didn't have to try to fit into any prescribed "pack", but was free to choose the friends that helped me be the person I wanted to be. By not feeling like I had to fit into any certain group, the trigger to be a mean girl was gone.*

I recently experienced mean girl behavior at my class reunion. I was first really surprised that at our age. our class mean girl was still trying to fit into the old high school pack. Then immediately, I felt very sad for her, I remembered how desperate and afraid I was to fit in, and all I could think was "what a horrible way to live". I hope she takes back her pen and her power..

Second: You create your experiences

The times when I behaved like a mean girl, I felt a little bit safe in the moment because I was protecting my status quo in the pack. But I also felt bad about the way I acted and what I had done. That bad feeling lasted much longer than the immediate bump of security I received. The energy I put out to that other person, I also experienced.

In the Bible, Jesus is quoted as saying "Do unto others as you would have them do unto you". I believe his intent is much deeper and is lost in this translation. I think the real message is "What you do to others you do to yourself." When you're mean to others, you feel bad. When you're good to others, you feel good. It really is that simple, and just like the first lesson, this one made me realize that I have the power to change my circumstances and I am not a victim to anyone.

Your circle should want you to win.
Your circle should clap the loudest
when you have good news.
If they don't, get a new circle.

CHAPTER**SEVEN**

What Gives You Strength?

The undercurrent of *mean girl* behavior stems from competition and comparison versus the strength of courage, confidence and compassion.

This story describes my point perfectly.

LESLIE & PEGGY STORY

Shortly after I posted the request for mean girls' stories on social media, Leslie responded saying she wanted to meet for coffee and maybe after talking to me she could finally put her mean girl story from 17 years ago behind her.

The surprising thing is that I barely know Leslie. She's more of an acquaintance, a friend of a friend. And yet, she wanted to tell me her story. She was willing to be vulnerable and trust me, even though we didn't have a strong relationship….

What if more women were willing to be vulnerable? AND what if they were treated with respect?

Our conversation began with some pleasant how are you, what have you been up to, general type of conversation.

I told Leslie when I first started writing my book it was going to be all about how to develop an inner circle. I wrote a few chapters and it was coming along. Then I started writing about what gets in the way of developing an inner circle with a focus of competition and comparison. As I started writing about these behaviors, I had a huge "Aha!" moment. The behavior that I was writing about was the typical mean girl behavior with which we as women are all too familiar. So much so that a woman can share just a few sentences about a mean girl experience with another woman and, in a matter of seconds, the other woman completely understands the entire event, because she has been there herself. I started writing about my own mean girl experiences and discovered a need to switch the book into two parts – the problem statement… Mean Girls, and the solution…: A Powerful Inner Circle. I realized the book should be written for women and not be the classic self-help with a corporate slant type of book, but instead focused on women with an intention of shifting our behavior. Instead of the norm being mean girls, shift the norm to inner circle behavior where women are welcoming, trusting, vulnerable, open and truly want to help each other achieve our dreams, instead of competing with each other. The next morning during my daily "10 minute" ritual of meditation, visioning and journaling, the answer was clear. The book will be written for women and it will be called, "Mean Girl No More!" with a tagline of "How to Shift from Sabotage to Support by Building an Inner Circle" This shift was heavy on my heart. It was so much bigger than me. I felt called to this work. Called to help women. Called to make a difference. Called to serve. AND scared at the same time!

As I told Leslie this story, she began to get emotional. She said she understood completely where I was coming from and could relate to everything that I shared. She agreed that there is a huge need for this type of work among women of every age.

I then asked her to tell me her story.

She was working in a dental office and was doing well as a surgical assistant. The doctors thought highly of her and complimented her routinely on being the best of the best. She was friends with the only RN in the office, and therefore the highest status, most responsibility and influence. Sadly, she was also a classic mean girl.

In the beginning, Leslie didn't recognize the behavior as being what it was. It was easy to turn a blind eye to it. When the RN didn't want someone to be on staff, she simply scheduled that person to work less and less. This, in turn, caused staff members to quit because they weren't getting enough hours. The RN did this over and over. In time, Leslie knew what was going on and chose to go along with it because she wanted to keep her friendship with the RN and, even though Leslie was ashamed to admit it, because things were going well for her.

The RN started planting seeds of doubt in Leslie about her pay in comparison to the other dental assistants. She disclosed that a new assistant was making more money which infuriated Leslie. One day, the RN and Leslie were in the locker area and everyone's checks had just been placed in their unlocked lockers. The RN said, "You know, Leslie, everyone's checks are in their lockers, you could look and no one would know." The RN, then on her way out, said, "I'll never know what you did."

Leslie bit the apple and looked in the new assistants' locker and discovered that she was being paid quite a bit more. She put the check away and met the RN for lunch. She disclosed she saw the check and the RN said, "I don't want to know anything about it."

Eight months later, Leslie went on a scheduled vacation to serve as a counselor at a youth camp. When she came back, everything had changed. She wasn't scheduled to work. When she asked about it, the RN said, "I just don't think you want to work anymore." Everything started unraveling. Before long, she was in a meeting with the two doctors and the RN and was fired. The RN had made up stories about her performance. Leslie was stunned. After all, she thought, they were friends and she hadn't done any of the things that were being said. She asked the RN, "Why are you doing this? You know me". The RN said, "Do you want me to tell them everything about you?" Leslie said, "Yes." The RN then used the paycheck story against her.

As Leslie shared this story with me, I could feel her pain, sorrow and anger. Even though it had been 17 years ago, the emotion was still there. She owned her mistake of looking at the check. She took full responsibility for her actions and even apologized to that assistant.

I asked her what bothered her the most and she stated it was because she didn't have closure. She couldn't explain her side of the story. She didn't want people thinking badly of her.

I shared with her, more often than not, we don't have closure from other people, but we can have closure from ourselves. We may want acceptance and approval from someone else to move forward, when all we really need is to forgive ourselves for our past behaviors, take the lesson we learned and apply it into our lives and accept ourselves.

I asked her what advice she had for a younger version of herself. Her response was powerful.

"Develop a healthy dose of self-confidence!"

If she had been more confident, she wouldn't have gone along with the mean girl behavior. She wouldn't have been afraid of not being friends with someone who was obviously hurting other people. She would have stood up for herself. In fact, with more confidence, her whole life would have been different.

Our conversation then shifted to what she's involved in today. I discovered she works with young women as a counselor in her church. She's in a position to influence these young women. Her experience and wisdom are being poured into others. I shared with her that I would be honored to share my book with this group of young women, to speak to them and help them learn why mean girl behavior happens and how to navigate it.

This is what happens when we're vulnerable with each other. When women join forces and trust one another, connection happens and that is when beautiful opportunities are created. I had no idea that this is what Leslie was involved in or how I could help her, until we met.

We began the meeting as acquaintances and left as women united to serve other women. What an incredibly powerful and beautiful future story.

COURAGE, CONFIDENCE AND COMPASSION

These three attributes are deeply connected. They are your kryptonite for dealing with a *mean girl* even if that *mean girl* is yourself.

It takes courage to go against the norm, to risk being ostracized and no longer be part of the pack. It takes courage to risk losing a relationship. It takes courage to speak your truth and it's the very thing you need to do to earn self-respect, which in turn, gives you confidence.

People who are self-confident do what they believe is right, even if they are mocked or criticized for it.

We earn self-respect when we listen to our inner voices and say the things out loud that are in our hearts and minds. When we voice our thoughts and feelings, even if they are difficult and unpopular, we earn self-respect.

Honoring our values and acting upon those beliefs in the face of adversity or risking approval of others can be difficult and is exactly what is needed to obtain self-respect.

It's when we disregard our inner voices that our self-respect erodes, and we begin to act "less than." Self-respect is knowing we are not less than others . . . instead we're equal. We are good enough to deserve love, happiness and success.

In case no one has ever told you, I'm telling you right now,

YOU ARE GOOD ENOUGH!

You are good enough to be treated with respect from others and, most importantly, from yourself.

Self–respect isn't thinking we're better than someone else or having a large ego. It's keeping a healthy balance and self-awareness of our short comings and our talents, capabilities, gifts and accomplishments. It's having enough self-confidence and self-respect that we can freely show respect to others.

I've been asked to coach people to help them build their confidence. I've been complimented about my confident approach and body language. And yet, I haven't always been as confident as I am now and, at times, I still struggle with being confident. I've been told by mentors and coaches that because of my confidence, I'll always be a target for other women, meaning *mean girls*. My confidence causes them to feel competitive and insecure and so they strike out. It hurts. It's confusing. More than anything, it's frustrating. I've learned over the years that this isn't about me. This is about them. When I hear, "She needs to stay in her own lane." Or "Who does she think she is?" it's easier to rise above it now than it was years ago. The reason is because I know exactly who I am. I'm living my life centered around my values and my purpose in this world. As silly as it may sound, I'm on a mission from God! I truly believe that, and it gives me strength. My confidence comes from this strength.

Confidence is one of our basic human needs. According to Maslow's hierarchy of needs, people need self-esteem derived from the respect of others, and from inner self-respect, and these needs must be fulfilled in order for an individual to grow and thrive. At the deepest level, it's about your belief system. Other than your actions and beliefs, the biggest factor in developing confidence is the relationship you have with the people closest to you. They either create confidence in you by challenging you to be courageous and creative, or they make you feel comfortable staying at the status quo.

Self-confidence is belief in yourself and your ability to influence yourself to live the life you desire. It's trusting in your own abilities and talents. It's knowing your purpose and living a life according to your values. If you have a healthy self-confidence, you're generally happier because you have the confidence to act upon your goals and that generally means you'll have more success in life. Each time you succeed, your confidence grows.

Confident people are healthier, happier, and more successful at coping. They have greater enjoyment in life, more energy to act and are relaxed. We all want these things in our lives, right? Here's how you get started: You practice being confident.

To build confidence, you have to practice confidence.

Confidence is not a personality trait! Confidence can be learned by:

1. Demonstrating Positive Body Language

The first step is to demonstrate confident body posture whether sitting or standing. If you aren't already familiar with Amy Cuddy, I encourage you to take 20 minutes to watch her TedX "Your body language may shape who you are." video. I promise you after you watch this, you'll know body language is powerful. It can boost feelings of confidence and make an impact on your success in life.

2. Practicing a Positive Mindset

For example, when a *mean girl* approaches you and attempts to tear you down, hoping to make you feel intimidated and unworthy, shift your mindset toward compassion for the *mean girl*. That's what a positive mindset looks like in action. In the beginning, this won't be natural, but over time you can make it a habit. You've been programming your mind for years to react a certain way in certain situations. You've essentially wired your brain to think a certain way for each situation you've gone through. Now, program your brain to choose a different path. Shift your feelings and thoughts. When you shift, your brain will get rewired to choose the alternate path.

3. Taking Care of Yourself

Do what you need to do to look good. When you look good, you feel good. When you look and feel good, people notice and think of you as being a confident person. It's your way to signal to people that you care enough about yourself to take care of yourself. Exercise has a powerful effect on confidence, even if it's a power walk. It doesn't have to be hours and hours at a gym. Exercise releases endorphins and those endorphins feed our brains with positive thoughts about ourselves.

4. Focusing on Your Goals

Achievement is the foundation of self-confidence. We'll talk more about this in the next chapter.

5. Practicing Positive Self-Talk

Can you imagine if we walked around with a microphone to our head that projected all our thoughts and what we say to ourselves? Most of us say worse things to ourselves about ourselves than we'd say to our worst enemy. We wouldn't even allow a *mean girl* to talk to us the same way we talk to ourselves.

6. Switching the channel from negative to positive.

Start talking to yourself as you would your best friend. Look at yourself in the mirror and tell yourself how proud, how beautiful, how smart, how good, how amazing you are. Build yourself up. Each and every time I'm feeling doubtful, I say something powerful to myself such as:

I am brilliant!

I am strong!

The first time you do this, it may feel strange and just like changing your mindset, over time it will become a habit. You'll be able to do it without thinking. It will be second nature. The key is to begin.

7. Collaborating with Others

Have you noticed how you feel when you get involved and help someone else? I've found when I give to someone else, it has a profound impact on my happiness. It creates a sense that we're part of something bigger than ourselves.

When we collaborate with others, our ideas are multiplied in ways we could never do on our own. The positive energy that comes from a collaborative effort has a powerful impact on our self-esteem and happiness.

Collaboration creates a sense of being valued by others and a sense of belonging. Invite others to collaborate with you. Be willing to give your time to others and help others on their journeys.

8. Embracing and Accepting the Process

Life is a journey, not a race. Push away the urge to compare yourself to others. Use your failures to develop yourself more fully. Instead of focusing on your mistakes, focus on what you learned from them. Stay focused on the journey. Yours is not a journey towards perfection. It's a journey on which, at times, you'll be a novice. At other times, you'll be a mentor. Breaking out of your comfort zone and starting something new expands your limiting beliefs and increases your capabilities.

9. Journaling the Journey

I've made it a habit to take the first 10 minutes of my day for me and my goals. Each morning I get up, get my coffee, go into my office and focus on me and my dreams. I have a vision board that I use for meditation. I imagine the life I want to live. I think. I dream. I'm in a prayerful, open state. Then, I journal my thoughts and feelings. Some days, I write about the accomplishments from yesterday. Other times, it's about my priorities for today. Some days, I write about how I'm feeling. Starting my day in this way fills my mind with positivity and confidence. I know where I'm going. I know why I'm here. I know who I am. This simple 10-minute routine is life changing.

Building a healthy self-confidence isn't a "check the box and you're done" activity. It's an ongoing journey. It takes time to build, develop and maintain. Begin tomorrow morning. You can use a plain sheet of paper, a spiral binder or a beautiful journal. You can write about whatever you want, whatever works for you, my only suggestion would be to make it positive. You can make a list of 3-5 things you're grateful for, you can make it a plan for the day. The most important thing is you take the first 10-30 minutes of your life for you and your dreams. You're dreams are worth 10 minutes, you're worth 10 minutes, so get started!

THE RUDY PRINCIPAL

One of the best pictures of confidence is in the famous football movie about the real-life story of Rudy Ruettiger. This young man had a dream and a vision for his life, AND the truth didn't matter. He had a dream of being a football giant and playing for the Notre Dame Fighting Irish football team. Imagine a young man who was only 5'6" and 164 pounds playing football when the average size of a Notre Dame player is 6'4" and 305 pounds, not to mention that it takes a GPA of 4.0. You've got to be at the top of your class! That, too, wasn't Rudy's reality. He had dyslexia and struggled in school.

In Rudy's mind, none of this mattered. All that mattered was his dream and how hard he was willing to work for it. He put in the work, and finally after the fourth try, he was accepted as a student at Notre Dame. This alone would have been an incredible success story. But Rudy never gave up.

He tried out for the football team as a walk-on player. He worked harder than anyone on the team. Each day, he was beaten and brutalized by a team of players almost double his size. That reality didn't matter to Rudy. He kept getting up each time he was tackled. He came back day after day, bruised and banged up more than anyone else on the team. Some of the players didn't appreciate how hard he was playing, started bullying him and asking him who he thought he was. They asked him what he was trying to prove. You see, he was working harder than anyone else and making some of them look lazy. He didn't have one friend on the team. He kept moving forward towards his dream any way.

His tenacity and heart ended up earning him a place on the practice squad, which is the team that helps the varsity team practice for games. His spirit was contagious. In time, he won over the entire team because of his spirit for the game and his passion for his dream. In Rudy's last opportunity to play for Notre

Dame at home, his coach put him into a game! AND in the final play of Rudy's senior year, he recorded a sack kickoff and was carried off the field by his teammates. To this day, only one other player in Notre Dame history has ever been carried off the field by his teammates.

The truth is, reality doesn't matter, here's what matters:

> How big is your dream and
> how hard are you willing to work?

When you know that you know that you know that you know what your purpose is in life – it's easier to let the toxic and negative behavior of the *mean girl* stay with the *mean girl* and not grab hold of you.

HOW TO DEVELOP COMPASSION FOR A *MEAN GIRL*

I've learned that *mean girls* are hurting. They're afraid, insecure, sad, and deeply wounded people. They're sick. They don't feel they have the power they need in their lives, so they are trying to establish power by hurting and controlling others. When you look at them with this mindset, you can develop compassion for them just as you would for someone who is sick.

When you look at them through eyes of compassion, you can put their words and behaviors into perspective. Your emotions will shift from feeling angry and hurt, to feeling sad for their state. This will give you the courage to handle the situation completely differently than if you feel you're competing with them and are afraid of retribution. This is not easy, but it's simple. You can make the shift.

In the next chapter, I'll teach you how to develop your confidence based around your personal values, the values that you bring to the table and your mission in this world.

If you could give this chapter of your life a name, what would it be?

CHAPTER**EIGHT**

Knowing Your Value

A lot us base our value on what we can do for other people. Or, we base it on what we were taught as a very young girl. Most women are raised to be good girls, good daughters, good granddaughters, good sisters, and good friends. We base our value on what others think of us or on how they perceive us.

Even as grown women, we're often still using this as the way to measure our value. We think if we're not good enough based on another person's perception, we aren't doing well and tell ourselves this limiting belief,

"You aren't good enough!"

This has to stop! Think about the compliments you hear from other women. Do they say complimentary things about a woman who takes great care of herself and is pursuing her dreams? Or, do they compliment a woman who sacrifices her self-care and dreams for her family?

We need to switch this up, ladies! Our daughters, our granddaughters, our friends, and even women who are complete strangers, need to see other women taking time for themselves, practicing great self-care and pursuing their dreams because... guess what happens...we make it OK for other women to take care of themselves and pursue their dreams.

Our influence is so much more powerful when we're an example of what we do rather than with only the use of words. When my daughter sees me pursuing my dreams at 50+, it makes a positive impact. It tells her she can pursue her dreams even though she's a single mom and a 20+ something young woman. I'm showing her that what it takes is time, work and effort. Self-imposed limits are within our minds and our value systems.

The way you make the switch is to recognize why you do the things you do and have confidence in the things you believe.

Why do you believe what you believe?

DREAM YOUR LIFE

Being ambitious shouldn't make you feel ashamed. You shouldn't have to apologize for going after your dreams. You don't need to fit into a box that someone else has created for you. You don't have to pursue your dream in a dark closet, hidden away from everyone, and in secret. You don't have to do it when everyone is sleeping. Think about it this way – do men struggle with this? NO! We, as women, shouldn't feel shame and anxiety for going after what we want in life either!

If your goal is to be a wife and stay-at-home-mom – fabulous! If you're married and have children and don't want to be a stay-at-home-mom – fabulous!

Why shouldn't we applaud and celebrate both?

The reality is both are valuable, worthy dreams. They both have meaning and are making a difference. Don't let anyone ever tell you anything different. The reason I'm so passionate about this is because I went through this same struggle of being a working mom and feeling guilty for it.

I remember hearing other women say, with demeaning tones and smiles on their faces, "Oh, you have a job. My family is most important to me. I put my children first. They're my #1 priority. I've chosen to sacrifice my career for my children."

What I'd like to say to women like this, isn't what I should write in this book because there's at least one four letter word that is conjured up in my head over these types of conversations.

What I think I muttered out at the time of being a young 20+ something mom and not having a choice but to work so that I could provide for my family, was something like: "It must be nice to have a choice."

The reality is that when things aren't going well, when you're at rock bottom, those women aren't going to be there for you to take care of the situation, they're not going to pay your bills, so stop letting them determine your value.

We need to stop this cycle of making working moms or stay-at-home-moms guilty for their lives. Our value shouldn't be about whether we're in the right box or if we fit in. Our value should be based on our own personal values, beliefs and dreams.

In order for you to create an inner circle – you need to know your values. There are two types of values: the value that you bring to the table and your personal values.

DISCOVERING YOUR VALUE

Most of us struggle with tooting our own horns or bragging about our strengths. Women, especially, shy away from this. Think about how you responded when someone asked you what your strengths were. Did you readily answer the question? Or, did fear set in and worry of rejection silence your answer? Have you noticed how readily men answer this question?

Think about the last time you were complimented; how did you respond? Did you say thank you, which, by the way, is the perfect response, or did you reject the compliment by saying something like, "Oh, this old dress, I've had this for years!"

The truth is we all have unique sets of gifts and talents that only we possess. Others may have something similar, but not exactly like you. Your talents, gifts, capabilities, experiences, perceptions, thoughts and dreams are what make you truly a one-of-a-kind individual.

"The world really needs that special
gift that *only* you have."
- Marie Forleo

See https://tinyurl.com/y2us6bwc and print this valuable worksheet.

YOU BRING VALUE TO YOUR INNER CIRCLE

To get you started on discovering the value you bring to the table, which is the same value you can give to your inner circle, answer these two powerful questions:

1. What lights you up?

2. What would you do even if you weren't being paid to do it?

The answers to these questions are your gifts. This is your brilliance that only you have. It's based on your experiences, talents and knowledge. This is the power you bring to your inner circle! To help you dig deeper and really nail the answer to what makes you valuable, schedule some time to really think through and answer these ten questions.

1. What did your teachers say about your strengths and potential?

2. How do your best friends and others describe you?

3. What does your boss praise you for in your annual review?

4. What do people say when they compliment you?

5. What do people ask you to be involved in as a contributor?

6. What's difficult or important about what you do?

7. What do you consider to be your highest contribution to the most important people in your life?

8. If you had unlimited time and resources and knew you couldn't fail, what would you choose to do?

9. What are your natural talents and gifts?

10. What do you really love to do?

We're each blessed with unique gifts and talents. You included! Keep digging until you know with certainty the value that you can bring to your inner circle.

Developing a powerful inner circle is built on you representing your authentic self. This isn't about pretending to be someone you're not. Trust and transparency are needed for a powerful inner circle to thrive. *This is so important.* You need to be secure enough in who you are and love yourself enough to know without any doubts that you have valuable gifts to offer – no matter who you meet.

What I mean is you'll likely come across someone who you look up to and admire and because of that you may doubt your own greatness. You'll judge yourself and think you don't have anything to offer. This isn't true. We all have something to offer each other, if we're willing to humble ourselves and learn from each other.

To help you nail this, so that you'll never doubt what you have to offer again, I've got an exercise for you that I was taught by one of my former coaches, JuliAnn Stitick. Here's what you need to do:

- Ask five people to be objective and, using five adjectives, describe you. You can ask whoever you want. They can be people you work with or you've done business with. They can be your clients or acquaintances. You can even ask your family and friends. The only requirement is that they're objective.

- Send a simple email like the one below to your trusted sources.

Dear Friend/Colleague.

I'm reaching out to you in the hope of getting some feedback on how you experience me as a person. Will you do a quick brainstorm and come up with five words that best describe me?

Your input is valuable to me. Thanks so much for your time and insight.

Sincerely.

You

- Then, take the results and create a poster of all those beautiful descriptions of you. Hang it somewhere you'll see it often and be reminded of the amazing person you are!

I hired a graphic designer to create a beautiful piece of art with the words people used to describe me. It hangs on the wall in my home office, right in front of my desk where I can easily see it. I look at it often and am reminded of positive ways people think of me. It's incredibly helpful to be reminded of these positive thoughts when I'm in the middle of difficulty and challenges, when I am not where I want to be, when I feel doubtful, when I'm about to make a huge negotiation, and even while writing this book! You could do the same or make your own, if you'd like.

I encourage you to follow through on all three of these steps, so you'll have something to anchor to in moments of challenge.

All too often, we don't see our own brilliance, especially women. Take these exercises seriously enough to discover the value you bring to your inner circle.

The more centered you can be about your purpose and your value, the more you'll have to offer. Here's what I know for certain: there are people waiting for you to show up and become part of their inner circle. *How long are you going to keep them waiting?*

DISCOVERING YOUR PERSONAL VALUES

(Please visit https://tinyurl.com/y59mgk6r)

Your values are your guiding principles. They drive your behaviors to help you make your day-to-day choices. They are at your core and are rooted deep down inside of you. They move you and help you discern what is your right from your wrong.

Ultimately, it's your values that shape your actions and your lives. The goal is to live a life aligned to what really matters to you. It's easy to get off track and be pulled in a completely different direction. We're inundated with information and marketing. Think about the amount of pop-up ads that appear while you're online or on social media. It seems Alexa is always listening. We mention something at the dinner table and the next time we pick up our phone or go online, "Surprise!" That very item is being sold to us!

Whether you've never done a values exercise before or you want to re-discover your values, I encourage you to take this step.

1. Look through the list of values below and circle the words that most influence your day-to-day choices and resonate the most with you. These words represent your guiding principles, standards and beliefs.

2. Review the values you've circled. There is no need to discard any of your choices. Imagine you're now in the middle of a difficult situation, or a wake-up call. It's time to get focused and prioritize your most important values. Narrow your list to six values.

3. Now rank your six values in order of significance. Again, you're not discarding any values. You're determining what rises to the top. The reason you're prioritizing your values is to prepare you for difficult decisions. Tough decisions are best made

when we're aligned to our values. Don't overthink the process; continue to let your core guide your choices.

- Abundance
- Acceptance
- Accomplishment
- Accountability
- Achievement
- Adventure
- Alignment
- Authenticity
- Beauty
- Challenge
- Charity
- Cleanliness
- Collaboration
- Community
- Compassion
- Connection
- Consciousness
- Consideration
- Contentment
- Contribution
- Cooperation
- Courage
- Creativity
- Decisiveness
- Dependability
- Dignity
- Direct
- Discipline
- Discovery
- Diversity
- Economic Security
- Education
- Effectiveness
- Elegance
- Emotional Well-being
- Empathy
- Encouragement
- Energy
- Enlightenment

- Entertainment
- Environment
- Equality
- Ethics/Ethical
- Excellence
- Experience
- Experiment
- Expertise
- Fairness
- Faith
- Fame
- Family
- Fitness
- Freedom
- Friendship
- Fun
- Generosity
- Global View
- Grace
- Gratitude
- Happiness
- Harmony

- Health
- Honesty
- Honor
- Hope
- Humility
- Imagination
- Improvement
- Independence
- Influence
- Information
- Inner peace
- Innovation
- Inspiration
- Integrity
- Intelligence
- Inventiveness
- Joy
- Justice
- Kindness
- Knowledge
- Laughter
- Leadership

- Learning
- Love
- Loyalty
- Magnificence
- Mastery
- Nobility
- Nurturance
- Observation
- Organization
- Openness
- Originality
- Peacefulness
- Perception
- Personal Development
- Play
- Pleasure
- Positive attitude
- Power
- Preparation
- Presence
- Proficiency

- Provider
- Quest
- Recognition
- Relationships
- Relaxation
- Reliability
- Respect
- Responsibility
- Results Oriented
- Risk
- Safety
- Self-awareness
- Self-worth
- Sensuality
- Service
- Simplicity
- Spirituality
- Stability
- Strength
- Success
- Superiority
- Support

- Teaching
- Teamwork
- Tenderness
- Touch
- Tradition
- Tranquility
- Trust

- Truthfulness
- Unity
- Victory
- Vision
- Wealth
- Wisdom
- Work Ethic

My Top Six Values

Priority/Rank

1.

2.

3.

4.

5.

6.

WHAT IS YOUR PERSONAL MISSION STATEMENT?

You've probably seen mission statements everywhere. They are on websites, in lobbies and on buildings. What you may not know is a mission statement isn't only for big companies. You can have your own personal mission statement.

In my first Executive Assistant position, I had the opportunity to attend a Leadership Team Workshop with our management team. The consultant had us each create our own personal mission statement. What I created all those years ago has stayed with me to this day,

I empower others to be successful.

A mission statement combined with your personal values and knowing your value will keep you focused and grounded. It pulls you back to what's truly important and why you're on this planet. A mission statement defines who you are as a person, identifies your purpose, explains how you're going to get there and why it matters to you.

Creating your personal mission statement takes time and should be given effort. It's a quick statement about who you are, where you're going and should inspire and motivate you.

Author and career coach, Dan Miller, says a good mission statement should include three things:

Your skills and abilities (What you like to do)

Your personality traits (How you operate)

Your values, dreams and passions (Why you want to excel)

That's it! It should be one or two sentences which say in simple terms exactly what you're all about without any principles tacked on.

According to the Forbes Coaches Council, there are 13 ways to create a strong personal mission statement.

1. Choose Your Path

2. Aim High

3. Be True to Yourself and The Future You Want

4. Find Your Core

5. Write Your Own Obituary

6. Define Your Impact

7. Stay Focused on Your Envisioned Future

8. Use the Verb-Target-Outcome System

9. Keep It Short and Sweet

10. You Already Know It

11. Go Through Your List and Ask "Why?"

12. Get Clarity on Your Values, Vision, Mission and Purpose

13. Be Honest with Yourself

When your personal mission statement, values, focus and actions are aligned – you'll have tremendous self-respect and genuine happiness. A personal mission statement keeps you focused on your goals. It serves as a massive virtual billboard guiding you to where you want to go in life. I'm telling you from experience, mission statements work! They keep you from wandering off track and going down detours. A personal mission statement is a tool for making tough decisions and setting boundaries.

Here's how you get started on writing your personal mission statement.

Set aside at least an hour and go through my goal worksheet. Please go to https://tinyurl.com/y4q2l7ch and print this form.

Then ask yourself these five powerful questions:

1. Why did you set these goals?

2. How do your goals make you a better person?

3. What is important – what and who do you value?

4. What does the best look like for you?

5. What kind of legacy do you want to leave behind?

In 50 words or less, summarize your answer to these questions. Get to the heart of who you are and be as brief as possible.

Once your mission statement is complete, print it, frame it and display it proudly. Include it in your bio. Share it with the people who are most important to you. Ask for feedback and accountability. You want people to know where you're going, plus it will help you live up to what you wrote. Your mission statement may change as you grow and develop. It's okay to make changes.

This story reminds me how important it's to know your value, to have a clear understanding of who you are so that you can move past the *mean girls* that may come into your life.

I CHOOSE TO REMAIN ANONYMOUS, PLEASE.

I had an interview for an Admin position for a company I had worked for before, but at a different location. I was well qualified, had my glowing letters of recommendation, certifications, etc. but something happened. I was called into the interview by the lead Admin for the company with as much warmth as a pit viper ready to strike. I didn't get it, I had never met her before.

I am a friendly outgoing person. It was really odd. During the interview I felt like I was in front of a firing squad. As a general rule, I interview well. I just didn't understand what was happening. I didn't piece it all together until much later.

A woman I worked with before had just started working there. When she worked with me before, I followed her taking over her old position. As a way of showing respect to her, I would run things by her for her opinion. After all, she had done the job before me. I would say things like, I was thinking about doing it like this, does that sound reasonable? It wasn't frequently, just enough to show her I valued her knowledge.

She left and I took over the HR responsibilities. Because she trained me, my manager must have asked her for input into my first evaluation. I found it in my file. It said, "She would not know how to do anything by herself if her life depended on it. She asks me about every little thing." I read that and was so angry because it was so untrue.

It was then that I realized how some people blow your candle out to make theirs burn brighter. It was a very sad lesson. I am sure in my bones the reason I was treated so badly before and during the initial interview was because they must have asked her about me and she told them things that weren't true.

I didn't get that job, but I ended up getting a job for a lower level Admin position much later. I applied for promotions, but never got an interview in over 30 attempts! I was blacklisted by the Lead Admin from the first interview in moving up anywhere in the company.

It has been five long years putting up with things I never should have had to. I finally worked with a group that saw my potential and I have been promoted to an exempt position and don't have to deal with those women again. You know it's bad, when correcting typographical errors on a shared admin website, lands you in an investigation for harassment.

I learned my lesson. Mean backbiting women exist. It's a sad fact. I wish more women were like me, always looking for the good and lifting other women up rather than tearing them down. We have enough obstacles in life, other women shouldn't be one of them.

ULTIMATELY, WHAT I'M ASKING YOU TO DO IS TAKE OWNERSHIP OF YOUR LIFE.

Complete the goals worksheet, discover or rediscover your values, and create your personal mission statement. These are the things you believe in and value. These are the goals you want to achieve. Own it! Move forward. This is what it takes to achieve your goals. This is it. There's nothing more to it. It's straightforward and simple. These are the same steps I've used to become a published author and professional international speaker. This method will work for you – you just have to do the work.

You can evolve and become the woman you want to be without guilt, without sacrificing who you are, and without feeling like you're a horrible mother, wife, friend, sister, daughter. It's easier to move forward in your life when you decide you no longer need approval from other people and not everyone has to like you. When we stand up for who we are, some people are going to love us, and some people will hate us. Some people will want to join you, others will want to distance themselves from you AND that is 100% completely okay because it's worth the risk to live a life you were designed to live. You'll be able to come out of your dream closet and into the daylight and boldly say who you are and what you're all about.

How would your life have been if you weren't trying to fit into a box since you were in middle school, high school, in your 20's, 30's, 40's, 50's……. What if you were told from a young age that you can be whoever you want to be, you have permission to be yourself and dream the dreams that make your heart soar. No matter how different that version of yourself is from others in your family, your class or your neighborhood it's okay. What type of confidence would you have from that experience? What if that was the norm?

My purpose for this book is to write about the real stuff, to share real stories and situations with the intention to shift the culture of women so that we can raise up ourselves and those who come after us. My dream is for women to no longer hold our self or others back and, instead, lift each other up.

Will you join me?

CHAPTER**NINE**

An Inner Circle in Action

Let me describe for you what a powerful inner circle looks like in action. When you have an inner circle, you have a group of people who are there for you, have your back in good times and bad, during the highs and the lows. This is the group of people who:

- support you and challenge you to move forward,

- love you enough to give you a kick when you need one,

- will tell you the truth even when it's difficult to hear,

- see your brilliance and all your potential, probably even more than you do,

- encourage and empower you to be the best you can be.

An inner circle is a group of people who are mentoring one another. It isn't about a relationship where someone is better than someone else. Quite the opposite. Each person in your inner circle is giving and receiving, teaching and learning.

The purpose of an inner circle is to share:

- knowledge,

- skills,

- information,

- perspective

- and foster personal and professional growth.

When you have an inner circle: you don't have to worry about comparison, competition and judgment; you're confident enough to know that when you surround yourself with others who are confident, it raises your game; and, you're smart enough to know that when someone else wins, it doesn't dull your brilliance. It's simply their time to shine. So, shine the spotlight on them!

Instead of comparison, competition and judgement, you trust each person in your inner circle. You let your guard down and share your innermost thoughts, fears and dreams with each other. You're vulnerable with each other. You strategize, philosophize and brainstorm to solve the problems in your life and theirs. You're open to their ideas and suggestions because you trust and respect each other. You know without any doubts that their intentions are to help you and never to hurt you.

When someone allows you into her inner circle,
the unspoken agreement is
that you don't abuse the proximity.

Take for example, my mastermind group (which has become one of my closest inner circles). There are four of us: Chrissy, Julie, Lisa and me. We're united over the purpose of helping each other become more successful. We're a very eclectic group of women with different backgrounds, interests and talents. We're different ages and levels of education. We each have our own businesses and our own followers. We're all speakers, so we could be considered competitors, yet we're not. Why? Because we believe in the law of abundance instead of the law of scarcity. We know there's enough room in this world for each of us to be successful. We know each of us has a gift to give this world that is unique. We know that our audiences need more than one source, one speaker, or one book to help them grow. We know there are certain people who only one of us can reach. We believe in the power of our work and the value we bring to our clients and audiences. It's because of this mindset, we aren't competitive with each other. In fact, when an opportunity comes our way that we can't satisfy or if there's a speaker call for several speakers, our first thought is to share it with each other. We gladly refer each other to the potential opportunity. We also share in celebration and joy when we all get selected to speak at the same conference. It's our way of having our own mini retreat our inner circle reunion!

"There's a special place in heaven for women who support other women."
~ Shelley Zalis

Often, one of us has an idea which needs to be polished and adjusted to turn it into a brilliant idea, so we help each other. We brainstorm and share resources. We're not in competition or a place of fear, so there's no hesitation.

We share our concepts, speaking topics, our latest creative workshop exercises, and even our books that are in the creation stage without any fear of stealing, sabotage or reproduction. That is how high the trust and respect level is for each other!

Who wouldn't want this type of relationship?

Shockingly to me, there are competitors out there who advise us and warn us to think again before sharing that level of insight about our business with each other. The beautiful thing is that it works for us. We're better because of what we've shared, and we respect and honor each other. Fear and worry doesn't exist in an inner circle.

What's really incredible is we didn't even all know each other when we first came together. Chrissy had the idea of forming a mastermind group with speakers. Chrissy knew Julie and she shared the idea with her. Julie knew of Lisa and me. Chrissy asked Julie to reach out to us to consider joining this speaker mastermind group. We all said, "YES!" and we've been together now for over a year.

There's rarely a week that goes by when we don't share something with each other. Whether it's a quick note of gratitude, a request for help, or a moment of celebration.

We have a scheduled bi-monthly call and also reach out to each other as needed for a particular topic or to bounce an idea off each other. Having a group of supportive people who truly care about each other and freely share knowledge and advice is a rare gift and one we all deeply respect and truly treasure. AND it's a true demonstration of an inner circle.

Can you imagine having this type of support in your life?
What would change in your life if you had an inner circle?

I love how the book, *The Female Hustlers,* described an inner circle in action.

Support your friends.

Listen to their ideas.

Go to their events.

Share their posts.

Celebrate in their victories and

remind them of their importance

after their failures.

A little support can go a very long way in someone's life.

When the competition, comparison, judgement and overall *mean girl* behavior is removed, it's so much easier to demonstrate these strong positive, powerful behaviors.

It's when we're fearful and insecure that it's difficult to provide support to someone else, especially to another woman who is doing really well. It's the strangest phenomenon. When you're tired and stressed out, it's easy to give an excuse of why you can't show up for one of your friend's events, especially when you may not know a soul there! When we aren't feeling confident, it's challenging to share a post or to offer a celebratory message to a friend who just reached her goal.

The lack of these positive powerful inner circle behaviors is so accepted that we even make excuses for each other when our friends and family, the people closest to us, don't show or praise when we've hit a home run. Right? We say things like, "Oh she's really busy. It's just not her thing. It's okay, I'm not that great anyway."

We tell ourselves that the lack of support in action is a result of our expectations being too high. We dismiss our talent and make up excuses for whoever failed to show up. We do this outwardly, but inwardly we're screaming, "Why aren't you here? Don't you value me? I need you. I need your support and positive energy."

How did this non-supportive behavior become the status quo?
Why do we accept this behavior as normal?

My goal since 2010 has been to quit my day job and be a full-time speaker, author and coach. It's been a journey and it most certainly hasn't happened overnight! Each year, my business continues to grow, and I've become a better speaker and coach. Experience is the master teacher. There's nothing better than having someone come up to you after you've finished speaking to say, "Wow, I saw you two years ago and man oh man, you've really grown!" It's somewhat of a compliment with a slap, but I understand where they're coming from.

I remember working for two different clients and within a short period of time they both told me the reason they hired me is because I'm still working full time in my day job. At first, it felt like an even bigger slap than hearing how horrible I must have been two years ago.

I asked each client a few clarifying questions to understand where they were coming from and learned they felt the reason I knew how to help them and knew what they needed is because I'm in their world. I took it as a sign from the Universe that I would never be able to quit my day job and I needed to continue to work both my full-time job and my speaking/coaching business. This basically means I have two demanding jobs. As you can imagine, it isn't easy! I wanted to scream, "Seriously! How can I sustain both for the next 10-20 years?"

A few weeks later, I was speaking at a conference and had a great conversation with one of the fellow speakers, who happens to be in my inner circle. I told her about the feedback I received from my two clients.

It was the shortest coaching session ever.

She simply took a deep breath, hung her head, looked me directly in the eye and shook her head no. She then grabbed a pen and paper and wrote,

"Think Bigger!"

Her message was profound! It was gripping! It was memorable! She said, "The truth is you'll never lose all your years of experience and the reason why you understand your client's world and know what they need is because of all those years of experience. It's those years of experience that caused you to have the wisdom, knowledge and experiences to share and teach others." She was telling me to get out of my own way. She was lifting me up and letting me know she saw me bigger than I saw myself.

You know where that note is now? Taped to my desk, right beside my computer monitor with a picture of a speaker in the largest sports arena I've ever seen and speaking to a sold-out crowd. I see this, "Think Bigger" message every day and I see myself on that stage speaking to a sold-out crowd and being mesmerizing, actionable and life-changing!

This is what a powerful inner circle looks like in action. Thank you, Melissa!

STANDING TOGETHER

When we stand alone, we have power. When we stand together our power and impact are multiplied—you need others and you need to invite them into your inner circle. The people in your inner circle see the real you. Not the perfect you on social media. Not the after makeup and perfectly put together you. The raw you, the 4am version of you when you're tired and messy. Who gets to see the real you? Who gets to see you while you're still becoming the woman you were meant to become? Without your inner circle, you can't complete your purpose.

People in your inner circle will give it to you straight. These are the people who have your back. Imagine what it feels like when you have a *mean girl* attacking you. You can only see them coming from one direction. But if someone has come alongside you and you're standing back to back then you can see the enemy coming. You'll be able to protect yourself and your dreams. There are people meant to be invited into your inner circle for this very purpose. People who have your back. This isn't about seeing eye to eye on every topic, it's about seeing what you can't see. We all have a blind spot, an area of us that we cannot see. But an inner circle can see your blind spot and because the relationship is built on trust, vulnerability and connection and positivity, they can tell you what you need to hear. They won't even wait to be asked to give you feedback. They have access to you and you've agreed to be there to help each other, which means you need to tell the truth to each other.

I told you about Debbie earlier—she's the one I told that I wanted to be a speaker while sitting next to her at my first large conference. Debbie has given me feedback on several occasions. One of the most memorable moments was when I accepted a job as a chief executive assistant—the highest position I had ever held. I was ecstatic to be selected, but after working there for a few months, I began to doubt my decision. I called Debbie and began telling her that I thought I had made a mistake on accepting this position. She asked why and then I went into full on pity party. I told her that I hadn't created a strong partnership with my boss, I hadn't figured out all the business systems, acronyms, clients, staff, campus, etc. etc. etc. When I finally finished, she simply said, "Oh you thought you were that good! You thought you could just walk into this huge job and nail it in a few months."

It was the perfect feedback and exactly what I needed to hear. It was the slap of truth I needed to wake me up and get me back on track. We all need someone that has our back and is willing to show us our blind spots and our strengths. Without feedback, your growth is limited. Your inner circle are people who will give it to you straight. They'll help you find your purpose and maximize your gifts.

The outdated strategies of competition and *mean girl* behavior no longer work. The truth is raising each other up and coming together collaboratively is what works. This is how we'll push through outdated ways of thinking and create a new normal.

There's a ton of research about powerful positive inner circles. Every piece of research I've read proves that women who support other women are more successful and happier. The *Harvard Business Review* states that women who have an inner circle are higher paid than those who don't. A study by the *Industrial Psychiatry Journal* suggests that female relationships are key to happiness and overcoming depression. Need more reasons to build a powerful inner circle? An inner circle of women will extend your life expectancy and lower your risk for heart disease! Talk about the *power* of an inner circle!

When you have a powerful inner circle, you have a group of people you can call on in your time of need, AND sometimes, you don't even have to call, they just somehow know when to call you or to show up! You may be in a full-on crises mode and haven't even reached out to anyone when you get a text, email, or a call from someone in your inner circle who says she was thinking about you and wondering how you're doing. Have you ever had that happen? You're thinking about someone and she calls you? This happens because of the power of connection. The energy is so close between you and that person that you feel each other even when you aren't in the same room. All of a sudden, you have a thought that you should call someone you care about. You might refer to it as intuition or energy, whatever you want to name it – all I know is, it happens!

Holly is that type of person. She's the one who I call when I'm in a bind and need a helping hand. She's willing to step in and do pretty much anything. She offers to help before I even ask. She's helped me paint my office, find the outfit that makes me feel amazing for a big event, put on a baby shower for my daughter and even make gifts for my workshops! You name it, she's probably done it for me.

What would happen in this world
if this was the normal behavior?
Can you imagine the culture shift if inner circle behavior
outnumbered mean girl behavior?
This is the exact reason I'm writing this book!

I must share this with you. It's too big, too important, too heavy on my heart not to share it with you. I told you earlier that this book wasn't my idea. My idea was to write a book with the entire focus on developing an inner circle, which has been my signature keynote talk and is a powerful message. It's one of my favorite topics. However, as I was writing my "Developing Your Inner Circle," book, my heart kept asking, "Should this book be written for women?" I kept pushing the question away, trying to stay focused on my original plan.

Each day, the question kept coming back, "Should this book be written for women?" No matter how hard I tried to stay focused and on my path for my original book, this question resurfaced, over and over again.

Then one day, during my morning ritual of coffee, visualizing, meditation/prayer and journaling, the answer became clear.

The reason women don't form an inner circle
is because of fear and pain
from their past experiences
and interactions with a mean girl.

I felt this overwhelming urge to let go of what I had planned for this book and, instead, write a book focused for women that shares stories that no one wants to talk about. The stories of how I've been a mean girl and how I've been intentionally hurt by other women. So, I started writing my stories, and they flowed out of me. I realized there were two parts to my book: a problem and a solution.

Problem: Mean Girl Behavior

Solution: Transform relationships by lifting each other up and forming inner circles.

I felt so strongly about this new path that I didn't even put up an argument about it, in short I gave up control. I knew that this was what I was supposed to do, what I've been called to do.

As I began writing my own stories, I thought it would be helpful for you to read about other women's stories. Without even hesitating about that thought, I posted a call on social media asking women to share their stories of mean girl experiences and the stories came rushing in. The stories flooded my inbox! It was like opening Pandora's box. It scared me. I didn't know where all this was headed, I just knew I had been called to talk about this area with the intention of healing women so that we could start coming together to lift each other up. My goal is that you and other women will use this book as a catalyst to start talking about what isn't being talked about – *mean girl* behavior and how we can change it. This book can be your tool to help you and other women move past their *mean girl* scars and move towards developing a powerful supportive inner circle.

When you keep feeling this tugging on your heart – that's God.

Sometimes, we can get so wrapped up around a goal that our hearts aren't even present – it's all in our heads. But, when you listen: when you pray and meditate; when you're still; you'll notice your heart is begging you to get out of your head and listen to your heart. Ladies - listen to where you're supposed to go and what you're on this planet to do! For me, this is it!

You are called to something – what is it?

All you have to do is take one single step toward what you've been called to do and be.

As you read this woman's story, imagine what an inner circle in action could have done to help her through this *mean girl* situation.

I am one of 16 "support staff". We all work in different departments, under different directors. I am fortunate to work in a department that encourages professional development and growth. I take advantage of that whenever I can. For whatever reason, this bothers my peers.

I never imagined at my age I would say that I was in a "bullying" situation. I've walked in the room and my peers, my equals, stop talking. I've been ignored when I was able to share something in a group that is exciting not just for me but for our profession. I've had eye rolls. I've heard that I need to remember my place. I've had things made up about me by people who I have no conversations with. I've been left out of lunches, peer group gatherings, after hours gatherings.

I have been recognized for accomplishments in front of entire staff, only to have my fellow support staff snicker. These instances have made me feel ashamed that I accomplished anything.

Sadly, I can't write this without sounding like the victim. I don't want to be a victim. I want everyone to be the best they can be. I want to share things I've learned and discovered. I've wondered why people that hold higher positions than me, continue to encourage and inspire me; however, my peers want to tear me down.

It's a daily affirmation for me to remind myself that I have too much going for me to let them take me down. I do distance myself from them and choose to surround myself with the coworkers that do encourage and inspire me.

I don't think I can say I have overcome it, but I am confident in saying that I know I do not deserve it; that I am a good person; that I do have lots to offer if they ever wanted to see me differently. Until then, I smile, kill with kindness, and focus on the many things I'm doing to be the best me.

Hear me loud and clear – you are loved, you are worthy, and you are good enough to pursue your dreams. It doesn't have to make sense to anyone but you. It can be so big that it scares you. You don't have to have everything figured out. Don't hesitate. Use your God given talents to be the women you're meant to be in this world. The world needs you. I need you. Your sister, your neighbor, your mom, your co-worker, your children, and your nieces need you!

There aren't enough women following their hearts. This world needs you to show up as your unique self, living the life you've been called to live.

I am the woman I am because of what I've walked through --- my past, my challenges, and my dreams. The time to choose your new path can happen whenever you want. It's not too late. You're not too old. You're not too young. You're not too inexperienced or over-qualified.

God uses each of us in beautiful ways, if we're open to it...even when it scares us, and when we weren't fully prepared for it to happen. I understand that God made me this way. I'm a driven woman. I have big dreams and goals. This desire is on my heart and I've been called to this work.

What about you?
What are you being called to do?

Once you discover what your purpose is, there's no reason to feel guilty anymore. Be 100% committed and step into it with boldness!

CHAPTER**TEN**

Connections
Create Happiness

"Connection is why we're here.
It's what gives purpose and meaning to our lives."
~ Brene Brown

A group of researchers from Harvard Medical School studied friendships and discovered that friendships make us feel good, so good that one person's happiness spreads beyond you and extends up to three degrees of separation and lasts as long as a year! Happiness is contagious! When we hang out with friends, the production of oxytocin, the feel-good hormone, increases. Oxytocin makes us more trusting, generous and friendly.

Study after study proves that having a positive inner circle is good for your health.

Researchers at Harvard linked depression and early death to a lack of strong friendships. Another study by scientists from Florida State University indicates that loneliness increases the likelihood of dementia.

It's smart to invest in friendships that make you happy. It's also smart to examine the relationships in your life. Consider the people who are closest to you: your family, your friends and your coworkers. How do you feel when you're with these people? After you spend time with your friends, do you walk away feeling upbeat, positive, inspired, encouraged and happy? Or, do you feel dark, depressed and filled with negativity? Do the people closest to you encourage you to be the best you can be? Or, do you feel the pull to stay in your comfort zone?

I encourage you to evaluate your relationships:

1. Make a list of the attributes that make you feel happy, safe, supported, inspired and encouraged to be your best self.

2. Make a list of the behaviors that cause you to feel negative, sad, depressed and discouraged.

3. Evaluate your relationships by looking at these two lists.

4. Evaluate your own behavior by looking at these two lists.

5. Determine if there are relationships that need to be improved or if it's time to exit a relationship.

This is a powerful evaluation process. Evaluating your relationships will illuminate the healthy relationships in your life and it will also shine light on the relationships that are dark, negative, toxic, discouraging and are ultimately holding you back. My advice is to create distance between you and those who cause you to feel the opposite of how you want to feel – even if they're family. You don't need to end your relationship with them, but you also don't need to spend a great deal of time with anyone who causes you to feel horrible about yourself and holds you back from your goals and dreams.

I've had to do this in my own life. It's not easy. It hurts when a family member isn't what we want them to be and when they don't meet our expectations or line up with the vision we created. Discovering this reality can be a hard one to swallow. I've learned we're all doing the best we can and if people aren't who we need or want them to be, it doesn't mean they are bad people. It means we can't put our high expectations on them and then feel sad when they don't live up to that vision or expectation.

I've also learned that you truly do become the five people you spend the most time with – it absolutely happens! If you hang around with people who are constantly criticizing other people and are negative, you'll sound and think like them. If you spend a lot of time with people who read and talk about what they've read, you'll start reading, too. We magnify what we're around. It happens without even thinking. So, my friends, choose your friends wisely, build a powerful inner circle of people who you want to emulate, people who you want to be like, people who lift you up.

Harvard did a study on adult development. It's the largest and longest study on happiness in existence. It began back in 1938 and was focused on what creates a healthy and happy life. There were originally 268 people in the study. By 2017, there were only 19 still living and all were in their 90's. The study expanded and included the children and wives of the original research group. When the researchers asked these people what they thought would make them happy, their responses were money, fame and achievement.

Interestingly, this isn't what created happiness. Here's what the study found:

"The surprising finding is that our relationships and how happy we are in our relationships has a powerful influence on our health," said Robert Waldinger, director of the study, a psychiatrist at Massachusetts General Hospital and a professor of psychiatry at

Harvard Medical School. "Taking care of your body is important but tending to your relationships is a form of self-care too. That, I think, is the revelation."

What makes us happy? Close relationships and having a powerful inner circle are essential to being happy and healthy. This isn't a numbers game of how many are in your inner circle. It's not about how many Facebook friends or LinkedIn connections you have. It's about having authentic relationships. It isn't about being married or not married. It's about nurturing yourself with relationships that are warm and loving.

You can feel lonely even when you're in a marriage or in the midst of a group of people. You'd be surprised to know that most people feel lonely, yet we're more connected than ever. Or are we? Just because you're connected on social media, are you really connecting with someone? We have all these Facebook friends and LinkedIn connections and yet have nobody to confide in, even though our social networks just keep growing and growing.

Loneliness is toxic and it leads to earlier illness, death and even erodes your mind. The US Surgeon General recently made a statement in the Harvard Business Review, "Loneliness is also associated with a greater risk of cardiovascular disease, dementia, depression and anxiety." Loneliness happens when you don't feel seen, when you don't feel a strong enough connection to feel safe and secure, when trust and vulnerability don't exist.

How fulfilling are your friendships on a scale of one to ten with ten being the most satisfying? How close do you feel with the five people that you spend the most time with? When I ask this question, the most common responses are five or below. The solution isn't about widening your circle, it's about choosing the right people and then taking the time to nurture the relationship. Developing authentic relationships takes time spent with each other to develop trust and once trust is built then you can be vulnerable with each other. When you have a powerful inner circle, you can feel connected even when you're all alone.

The people who were the most satisfied
in their relationships at age 50
were the healthiest at age 80.

I've been blessed to have married a wise and loving husband, Renè. He has taught me so much about life. He knows the greatest gifts he can give me are beautiful moments. He helps me lean into enjoying life. Renè has created so many incredible moments in my life. As Waldinger said, "A happy marriage will extend your life, your memory and your overall happiness."

When I'm 90 years old and my grandchild is on my lap, I'll still be telling stories of the wonderful adventures and incredible moments that I've experienced, largely because of Renè'.

Actually, the best gift you've given me
is a lifetime of adventures.

We've been married for over 34 years. Each year, we've become closer and closer and learned how to love one another more. Our love was there from the moment we met, but the richness of our love has continued to grow. It didn't happen overnight. It took time and effort to build a committed, loving relationship.

My dear friend Amy is someone that I've known even longer than my husband. We met in high school and are still close friends today. She's the person that will call or text when I need encouragement. She's got this incredible gift of wisdom and discernment. She's able to weed through all my excuses, doubts, fears and BS and figure out what's going on quickly. She asks just the right questions to help me discover what's at the heart of being stuck. Amy's got this great sense of humor and can quickly get me laughing over the situation and then at just the right time give me a dose of wisdom to build me up and push me towards my purpose.

Our relationship has been years in the making. We have stories, sayings and what sometimes feels like our own language. We can break into song because of a phrase someone spoke. We laugh as we reminisce about old stories and dream of new memories to create.

Building meaningful relationships isn't a quick fix.

Waldinger also said that our society is programmed for a quick fix. We live in this instant gratification society of food that is cooked in seconds, instead of hours. We can order groceries online and have them delivered to our homes. We can send a quick text message instead of taking the time to go visit someone or even call and talk to them. Instead of calling a friend or family member, we can post a message on social media as a way to keep everyone updated on our lives. This is not how you build a powerful inner circle or meaningful relationships.

Building relationship capital
requires a substantial investment.

Recently, I attended a large fundraiser. There were over 1000 people in the room and the majority were women. As I walked into the room, I was greeted with smile after smile - genuine smiles, the type that start at your heart. I immediately felt at ease and welcomed. As I looked around the large entrance way, I noticed this was happening all around me. I observed women approaching each other with the warmest smiles and hugging each other. I heard woman after woman complimenting each other on their hair, dress, and shoes. It was a contagious! It felt like a family reunion. It felt incredibly joyful. In short it was a powerful experience.

Do you want to walk into a networking event and be greeted by people with a warm smile, a hug, a word of encouragement and a compliment? Of course, you do! The only way that is going to happen is for you to start giving that type of welcoming behavior to others. It all begins with making a connection and then making the time to nourish that connection. Authentic, powerful connections, and having an inner circle isn't something that happens overnight, and it won't happen without making a conscious effort to build those types of connections. Meaningful relationships are built one moment at a time. If you want a powerful inner circle, you need to make it a priority.

THE TIME QUANDRY

I can already hear you, "I don't have time! My to-do list is already two feet long!" Take a deep breath. This isn't about time. It's about a conscious effort. Relationships can be built anywhere and at any time.

In fact, because of all the ways you can connect with someone electronically, they don't even have to be in the same room with you.

We all want the secret to time management . . . well, I'm here to tell you that work/life balance is a myth AND if you think otherwise, you're going to be sorely disappointed. It doesn't exist. We aren't split into three or five or ten different people. We're one person. While we're living our lives, we focus on different areas of our lives for different reasons. If you're new in your career, you're going to spend a lot more focus and time on your career. If you're a new mom, you're going to spend a lot of time and focus on your children. If you're moving into a new home, you're going to spend a ton of time getting moved into it. If you have an elderly mom who is terminally ill, you're going to spend an extraordinary amount of time with her. If you're engaged and your wedding date is coming up, you're going to spend every ounce of time you can find focused on creating your perfect wedding.

None of these choices are wrong or right.
They are simply the choices you make
based on that moment in time
and based on what matters most to you.

When you have the good fortune of a stress and crisis free life, your choices may look a little more balanced. Let me know how long that perfect moment of your life lasts!

In my life, I've had to make choices, some easy, some incredibly difficult and some that others didn't agree with. I've made choices that weren't popular.

My reality is I'm working full-time in a demanding job. I have a side hustle that is growing by leaps and bounds and is my dream career. I'm involved in my community both locally and internationally. And, I have an incredible family including a husband of 34 years, 4 children and 7 grandchildren, plus an amazing inner circle. My life is in hyper drive!

I'm often asked, "How do you have time to fit everything in? How do you work full time and have a successful speaking and coaching business and find time to write? How can you manage to find time for your family? How do you do it all?"

I always say, "I don't fit it all in! I simply make choices." You see, we all have 24 hours in each day. Everyone I know is busy and is doing their best to manage the competing priorities in their lives. Don't confuse busyness with moving towards your purpose. One of the highest purposes of an inner circle is to help you find and move towards your purpose. Life is complicated and complex. Life is about the choices we make and how we spend our 24 hours each day.

I have a powerful support group (my inner circle) that keeps me grounded:

#1 is my relationship with God, who loves me as my unique, beautiful, talented self. This relationship with God is about love. It's not about being part of a certain religion, praying through a person, acceptance from a human being or about judgment. It's about love, love, love.

#2 is my loving and supportive husband who has taken on more than his fair share to run our household and pulls me away from my work to enjoy life as I have a tendency to be a workaholic.

#3 is the amazing circle of friends that I've surrounded myself with who lift me up when I've failed, pick me up and, sometimes, kick me forward, give me advice and cheer my success.

#4 are my children and grandchildren who remind me of the simplicity of living life and who pull out unconditional love from the depths of my soul and enrich my life through their existence.

I practice a morning ritual of having a cup of coffee, taking my vitamins and getting into my private space to focus on my dreams, meditation, prayer, visualizing and journaling. This reminds me who I am, why I am here, where I'm going and what I'm feeling. The journey isn't about hitting the mark and celebrating. The journey is about each day of my life. Journaling reminds me about today, this day, not when I'm finished writing this book and the sweet victory of opening up the first box of books so I can see my dream in reality.

These habits are there each and every day regardless of what day of the week it's or if I'm on the road. This begins my day with an accomplishment. There's something magical about starting your day with a focus and accomplishment. It's a reminder of what I'm working toward. Those thoughts I had while meditating, visualizing and journaling will stay in my conscious and subconscious mind throughout the entire day. This simple habit of a morning ritual prepares me with a positive mindset ready to battle any negativity or challenge that comes my way.

If you own the morning,
You own the day.
Start your day with intention!

THE MAGIC OF HELLO

Want to know how to build connections? Learn how to say, "Hi!" It really is that simple. Start saying hello to people. Where? Everywhere! Connections can happen at any time, not only at networking events.

One of the biggest reasons that holds us back from going to a networking event is it sounds like work! After all, the word "work" is in the word networking.

Here's a likely scenario: We're at work doing our typical routine, when out of nowhere it hits us! We come across the dreaded invitation to a networking event! We quickly glance at our calendar, hoping we're booked. Panic sets in as we see we're wide open. Our blood pressure begins to rise, and we can feel the nervous energy building. Then our clever mind - immediately employs our best and brightest – our most creative and strategic thinking to find a way to decline....... Am I right?

Here's a typical decline response: "Thank you for your invitation. Due to previous commitments, I am not able to attend. I wish you much success at your upcoming event."

Like magic, we're off the hook! But, are we really? Did we luck out or miss out? When we miss out – we miss out on the opportunity to connect with others and to establish a relationship. The whole purpose of networking is to create authentic connections and develop relationships. You network every day. It's called talking and interacting with others.

Start saying hello to others wherever you are. See if the person in front of you, beside you, or behind you is someone you want to build a connection with or not. (Both of which are okay, by the way.) Connect where you can and if you can't, move on. Realize you'll meet people with whom you aren't going to want to connect based on their values, character and authenticity. That's okay. The reason we have networking events is to meet people. We don't have to spend the evening with someone we don't want to connect with. That's the beauty of networking. It's time to explore possibilities.

When you learn that you have a shared interest with someone, you'll likely want to connect. When you make meaningful connections, those relationships will last a lifetime.

I encourage you to put yourself in environments where you have the opportunity to meet with your peers, with new and old friends. I guarantee this will be a game changer for you. Without taking the time to discover other people, you'll never know how rich your life could have been, or how you could've helped each other… which would have made you more successful and, possibly, happier and healthier people.

Ultimately, you have to decide that time spent with your inner circle and time invested in building an inner circle is a priority.

"To make connections,
you first have to decide
if it's important to you"
~ Erica Keswin

CHAPTER**ELEVEN**

Build One Before You Need One

When is the right time to build a powerful inner circle?
Before you need one!

Have you seen the desperate behavior of someone who is unexpectedly out of a job and doesn't have an inner circle? There's nothing worse! You get a phone call out of the blue from someone you haven't heard from since high school asking you if you have any leads on a job and if you'll be a reference. They haven't built an inner circle, so they reach back to 10-30 years ago because that's all they have – their resource pool is limited, they haven't built any relationship capital to cash in at the time when it's really needed.

Take the opposite story—someone who has been building an inner circle for years and is unexpectedly out of a job. The sting of losing the job is still there, but there's comfort knowing you have a huge inner circle of people to call, not only for leads and referrals, but also for comfort and encouragement. Wise people take the time to invest in building relationship capital. They know there will be a day when they need it, so they make it a priority investment.

Which situation would you rather be in? During unexpected moments of loss and change, there's nothing like an inner circle to get you through the challenging situation.

*****

In my last book, NOT Just An Admin, I shared the story of Damon, my grandson, being diagnosed with leukemia when he was 18 months old. The fear and worry that flooded our minds when we heard the word "cancer" was overwhelming. It was a 3 ½ year treatment process and one of the most difficult journeys our family has faced. We're beyond thankful and blessed to say that Damon is now cancer free and is a thriving seven-year-old boy.

What got us through those nights of doubt and darkness as our baby grandson was fighting for his life other than our faith in God? We had the comfort of a huge inner circle around us who came together to support our family. This amazing group of people took it upon themselves to host and coordinate a large fundraising event for our children and grandson. We weren't involved in the slightest. People stepped up to help plan, decorate and provide auction items. The event was held in the middle of winter with an ice storm and the people in our inner circle showed up any way. When you've taken the time to build an inner circle, you can rest assured they'll be there for you, even in the midst of an ice storm!

How do you build an inner circle? Demonstrate behaviors that attract meaningful connections.

Attract what you expect,
Reflect what you desire,
Become what you respect,
And mirror what you admire.

Dale Carnegie got it right with these eight behaviors:

Don't criticize, condemn or complain - I promise you the more positive you speak and think, the more positive your relationships will be.

Give honest, sincere appreciation – The deepest principle in human nature is the craving to be appreciated. Give sincere appreciation to others.

Become genuinely interested in other people **- To be interesting, be interested.**

Smile. The simple action of smiling tells people you're approachable, friendly and trustworthy. When we smile, it triggers a sense of happiness. What happens when we smile at someone? We feel happier. Right? If you're struggling with your boss or coworkers, before walking into the office, pause and think of all the things you're thankful for and then you'll be able to smile sincerely.

Remember, a person's name is the sweetest and most important sound. So, use their names when you're talking to them. Often, after we're introduced to others, we can't remember their names. To remember people's names, repeat the name after they introduce themselves to you. Say the name several times during the conversation. If you have trouble picturing it, ask how to spell it.

Be a good listener. Encourage others to talk about themselves and their accomplishments. If you aspire to be a great conversationalist, then be a good listener.

Talk in terms of the other persons interests - Ask questions the other person will enjoy answering.

Make the other person feel important and do it sincerely. We all want recognition of our true worth, a feeling that we matter, and that we're important. Sincerely make others feel important. Give others the VIP treatment.

These eight suggestions are timeless. The key is to make these behaviors a habit. Incorporate these behaviors into your daily interactions with people. I promise you the more you demonstrate these behaviors, your ability to attract meaningful connections will increase dramatically! I can confidently make this promise because I've seen it happen time and time again. Begin today with one behavior at a time, then add in more until they become natural.

"Great people are those who make others feel
that they, too, can become great."
~ Mark Twain

I love the story of Ubuntu, told by Martha Beck.

"In rural South Africa, where most do not have the material resources that you and I enjoy, they could feel envy and resentment, and yet, they have an enormous sense of warmth and generosity. My African friends tell me this stems from their philosophical grounding in Ubuntu. The word, which has no direct English translation, essentially means "I am because we are."

Ubuntu reminds us that humans didn't become a dominant species by competing. We did it by cooperating. In small villages surrounded by threatening wild animals, each person is precious, and sharing brings abundance. If one villager learns a skill—say, a new way of growing food—she benefits more from teaching others than from using her knowledge to compete against them. When her neighbors thrive, they increase the group's collective resources; there's more for everyone, and the village is stronger as a whole."

This is such a beautiful philosophy, one that we, as women all over the world, should adopt. Can you imagine if the mindset of women, no matter where you lived was Ubuntu? We must start sharing our knowledge and opportunities with each other. We have to stop competing, comparing and criticizing and, instead, empower each other.

Empowered women – empower women!

What does empowering other women look like? It's moving away from the habitual negative behaviors of sabotage and into positive behaviors that support the success of each other. It's shifting our mindset from scarcity to abundance. It's having a healthy confidence that comes from knowing we're each valuable.

Here are a few scenarios to show the difference between a sabotage mindset and a supportive mindset:

Situation: My coworker is being considered for a promotion.

- Sabotage mindset: Share negative history, exaggerate to discredit and dishonor, all done with the intention of negatively persuading the decisionmaker.

- Support mindset: Share information and insights to positively affect the decision-maker. Give examples of person succeeding in a similar role to instill confidence.

Situation: My friend is getting more recognition than me.

- Sabotage mindset: Ignore the achievement. Don't join in the celebration or provide any type of recognition for accomplishment. Gossip and plant seeds of doubt about how she was able to reach her level of success. Belittle the accomplishment.

- Support mindset: Openly praise and demonstrate recognition for your friend in private and in public. Show up for award event, and if there isn't an event already planned, be the first to create the event. Shine the spotlight on your friend with confidence knowing her success doesn't dull your own brilliance.

Situation: My co-worker is a new mom and has recently come back to work.

- Sabotage mindset: Limit growth and leadership opportunities with this person because, after all, she won't have the time to commit to anything. Remind people that she is a new mom and not to ask her to contribute because she won't be able to handle the pressure.

- Support mindset: Share opportunities equally with your new mom co-worker just as you would if she wasn't a new mom and let her decide what she can or can't handle.

Sabotage Mindset

- Envy
- Jealousy
- Degrade
- Intimidate
- Criticize
- Demean
- Spread rumors
- Ostracize
- Scarcity

Support Mindset

- Generosity
- Admiring
- Dignify
- Encourage
- Coach

- Uplift
- Promote
- Embrace
- Abundance

It all begins with a conscious choice to react to situations differently. Instead of continuing with a negative sabotage mindset, begin to create new pathways in your brain that lead to empowering women. Your mind is wired based on your past behaviors. You can retrain your brain to think and act differently. It begins with one deliberate thought at a time. If you find yourself falling back into *mean girl* sabotaging behaviors, take a deep breath, stop and redirect towards supportive empowering behaviors.

Here's what positive support and empowerment looks like in action:

Champion – A champion is someone who sponsors you. This is beyond typical; it's having someone in your corner that advocates on your behalf. She recommends you, knows and share your strengths with others and influences others to share opportunities with you.

Mentor – A mentor is someone who guides you. She shares information and knowledge and gives you the opportunity to choose which way to go. She doesn't give you the answer because she knows that would limit your growth. Instead, she helps you discover options and gives you the security and reassurance to make your own decisions.

Include – Be the type of woman who invites others to join your inner circle. Welcome others to the table. Offer someone a seat at your table. This doesn't need to be a formal invitation, or it can be—that's completely up to you. The point is that you aren't creating cliques where some are welcome, and others aren't.

Encourage – Make a point to openly encourage other women. Most of us have enough challenges and stress in our lives. What we need is someone to encourage us and help us believe in ourselves. The last thing anyone needs is criticism and judgment. Encourage others to keep moving forward one moment at a time. Provide words of positivity to lift up someone who is struggling through a challenging situation. Send a handwritten card in the mail. Buy a small token of appreciation and wrap it beautifully, letting her know how much you care. Bring her favorite cup of coffee to work or pay for lunch. Sometimes, the smallest thing can turn someone's life around. We're all going through something. In fact, some of the people who may seem the most confident are often the ones struggling the most.

Shine the Spotlight – When your coworker, friend, colleague, or family member is getting recognized, be the first to show up and the last to leave. Shout and clap and give them a standing ovation. Sing their praises to others. Have the mindset that their accomplishment doesn't dim your brilliance; it's simply their time to shine, so shine the spotlight bright!

Speak up – When you see something that is wrong, even if it's not illegal, say something! We've all been there – we witness something that isn't right, and we ignore it out of fear. Being a *mean girl* isn't okay. Sabotaging someone isn't right. This negative behavior shouldn't be tolerated or ignored. Speak up. Call attention to the negative behavior.

When I tell women about my book and *mean girl* behavior, almost everyone responds with a deep heavy sigh of acknowledgement and a nod of the head indicating yes. It's this validation that we all know what it means, without even saying it out loud. We then talk about the negativity and toxic energy.

When I continue to share the concept of a powerful inner circle, they want to know more about what one looks like in action. I ask them to remember a time when they've been with a group of women who are united and how powerful that feels. They again nod their heads but say an exuberant, "Yes." They identify with these two behaviors immediately.

We have the power, as women, to turn this *mean girl* behavior around. If a group of women come together over a cause, look out! Somehow, we've convinced ourselves that we need men to empower us when, in fact, women are the answer. We are the solution. When women come together and make a stand, it's powerful! Let's band together so tightly that we can't be ignored. When women thrive, we all thrive! What I mean by this is that when a woman is successful, she immediately puts those resources back into her family and community. Women are natural care givers and it's instinctive for them to think of those they love and share their rewards with them.

"You cannot get through a single day
without having an impact on the world around you.
What you do makes a difference,
and you have to decide what kind of difference
you want to make."
~ Jane Goodall

CHAPTER**TWELVE**

Discover Your
Greatest Potential

"The only person you are destined to become
Is the person you decide to be."
~ Ralph Waldo Emerson

When I first created my inner circle, my main focus was on finding people who could lift me up and help me achieve my dreams and goals. As I continued on this journey, what I discovered was that achieving my goals wouldn't actually be my greatest blessing.

You see, we're wired to be connected to others. And, that connection is strengthened by making a positive difference in each other's lives. It isn't a one-sided benefit equation. It's coming along side another person and focusing on what you can do for them instead of only what they can do for you. The interesting phenomenon that happens as you mentor someone else is you grow in return. You can't teach someone without teaching yourself. You grow from the experience as the person you're mentoring grows. When you help someone by brainstorming and problem solving a particular challenge she is facing, you're both engaged in a learning experience. Each experience we have leads to the next and the next. It's these experiences that prepare us for our next challenge. It's a serendipity of having an inner circle.

The wisdom you gain along the way will serve you and others in the future.

Several years ago, I was asked to recruit and place a Human Resource Director with a financial planning organization. Selecting the right person for the job was a huge responsibility. They had never had an HR professional before and their organization needed that level of expertise to take them to the next level by creating a positive and professional culture. I was thrilled when the right person was selected. Within three years, she had turned the organization around and hit the CEO's goal of earning the award as one of the top places to work. She was thriving and the company was thriving…so well, in fact, they decided to eliminate her position! She made it look all too easy and gave them the impression the organization could now be in cruise control mode.

Shortly after receiving the news, she sent me a text. My heart sank. I was shocked and couldn't believe what she was texting me. I told her I would call her back as soon as I could get home from work, so that we could chat privately.

While driving home, I thought about what I could say to help lift her spirit and give her hope and encouragement. I prayed and asked God to guide me. I called her and simply started pouring love into her. The words were flowing out of my mouth. My heart was full of love and concern for her. I started lifting her up with sincere words of praise and honor, reaffirming she was talented and valuable. The words flowed effortlessly because they were coming from a Higher Power and they were beautiful, loving, powerful words.

There's no greater honor than lifting someone up when they are crushed, scared and feeling confused and powerless. Being in that vulnerable moment with her was because of the connection we created years ago. I was there for her and there was no doubt in my mind that God had us both in His hands to help each other.

Three days earlier, while on a call with a friend from my inner circle, she shared an experience of being fired years ago. At the time, she was crushed and confused. She had moved to another city to accept this job and felt with one hundred percent assurance that it was the right job for her. Why had she been led to this great job, if it wasn't meant to be the right job? Why was she being fired when she had been performing well? Question after question swirled in her mind. What she discovered is the great job she accepted caused her to move to another city. Leaving the old job behind was what she needed to do. It was the catalyst to get her to move and to propel her out of her comfort zone. Months went by without a new job. She was in the hallway of darkness, waiting for a door to open. That hallway is challenging it's dark; its long; and, often, you feel alone and confused. If you surrender to God, the Universe, a Higher Power – whatever you want to call it… if you surrender and ask for help – God will be there for you to guide you where you need to go, help you discover what you need to learn, hold you and walk with you through the hallway and find the right door to open. What happened next was she found her dream job…a job that wasn't on her radar in that same city to which she had moved. She had been led to the right city and to the right job. It took time. It wasn't an obvious choice, but it was the right path.

Hearing my friends' story is what prepared me for the phone call with my Human Resource Director friend. I had the right words to say that had been put into my heart and soul just three days before. This is the power of an inner circle.

We're all connected to each other. We can all help each other, if we're open to it.

Discovering your greatest potential
is about serving others.
How do you do that? By showing up!

It's easy to get into the trap of being too busy and too self-absorbed to want to serve. You can justify your actions by telling yourself that you would help but you simply don't have the time and a quick text back will do. Yet, you know in your heart this was the easy way out. Guilt eats at you because you know they needed you. Push past the laziness and selfish mindset. You're connected to each other for a reason and that reason is to help each other.

Each time you help someone, it lifts you up to a new level of understanding and wisdom that will someday help you or someone else navigate through a difficult challenge.

Do you think it was a coincidence that someone reached out to you? It wasn't a coincidence. It was an opportunity. Sure, it takes courage to act when you haven't done something before. But when you hesitate to act on an opportunity, you may very well miss the opportunity. Don't buy into the thoughts that you aren't prepared, this isn't the right time, and you don't have the knowledge or experience needed. This leads to being stuck in your comfortable life complaining that your life is the same-ol', same-ol'.

"We'll never know our full potential
unless we push ourselves to find it."
~ Travis Rice

You may hesitate because you don't feel ready or you don't have any expertise to handle the situation. The reality is, no one is ever ready. There are countless examples of this from Steve Jobs to Michael Jordon. Beyoncé has sold over 17 million albums and when she was 9 years old, she appeared on Star Search and lost. Bill Gates is one of the richest men in the world by developing the mega giant Microsoft, yet his first company failed miserably. The incredibly talented Fred Astaire, who had a reputation for shooting his famous dance scenes in one take, was rejected by a Hollywood producer stating, "Can't act. Slightly bald. Dances a little." Even the queen of talk show television, Oprah Winfrey, was fired and told she was unfit for TV!

> "There is no heavier burden
> than an unfulfilled potential."
> ~Charles Schulz

Fear is what keeps you stuck… fear of failing; fear of not knowing what door to open; and fear of not knowing what to do or say. The truth is, I've never met a successful person who didn't face some fear. Think of any successful CEO, athlete, artist, author, assistant, or parent you know. Did this person know what to do on day one? Was she ready to handle each new situation that came her way? NO! She did the best she could with what she had and learned along the way. With each mistake, she learned and got better and became the success story she is today. That success did not happen overnight. It took time, just as discovering your greatest potential will for you. Successful people do things before they're ready. They raise their hands and step up to the challenge.

The first step is to say "yes" when the opportunity comes, then figure out "how" along the way.

"When we least expect it, life sets us a challenge to test our courage and willingness to change; at such a moment, there is no point in pretending that nothing has happened or in saying that we are not yet ready. The challenge will not wait. Life does not look back. A week is more than enough time for us to decide whether or not to accept our destiny."
~ Paulo Coelho

When I began my speaking career, I was far from ready. I didn't have any experience. I relied on my passion and enthusiasm to become a speaker. I paid attention to other speakers who I admired. When I attended training, I took notes about the content in the middle of the page and in the margin, I made notes about what the speakers did. Things like pace, intro, how they segued from one point to the next, what their slides looked like, what they wore, and how the audience reacted. I was a student who absorbed and observed everything. I was preparing for the opportunity. So, when the opportunity came, I was ready. Truth be told, the first two times I spoke, I wasn't asked to speak. I asked for the opportunity and because I asked, the opportunity was created.

Stop waiting to be asked, create your own opportunities! What's the worst that can happen? Maybe, you'll get a "No."

Getting a "No" stings. Dealing with rejection is one of the hardest things to overcome. No matter what business you're in, rejection is part of business. You offer ideas for a project, you create proposals, you share an idea, you pitch a new approach all in hopes to get to a yes. Getting a "Yes" feels like validation and acceptance that your work is good enough to be selected. Sooner or later, everyone gets a "No" and "No", isn't always a rejection. It simply means, "No, thank you. Not now." Think of it this way, when you're at a restaurant and the waiter asks you if you want ketchup and you say no, does she run away crying and feeling rejected? There are times you may get rejected because there is an even greater opportunity coming. You may have received a no because you have work to do, which isn't necessarily a bad encounter. It may sting but it's also valuable feedback. Your content, ideas or pitch may need to be refreshed or you may need to develop something completely new.

Reframing is key to staying on track
to discover your greatest potential.

Buying into validation by getting approval and acceptance from others is a wicked trap. It can lead to relying on others for your self-esteem and self-confidence. Discovering your full potential isn't about what others think of you. It's knowing your talent and generously giving it to others. It's meeting a need, solving a problem and shifting someone's mindset. It's enriching lives. It's doing what you're called to do to make the world a better place because you were brave enough to put yourself out there – ready or not!

Shortly after I wrote my first book, I landed head-first into the trap of acceptance and approval from others. Writing a book is flat-out challenging. It takes time away from the easy life of zoning out on Netflix and relaxing on the sofa. It requires a continuous effort. It takes pushing past the feelings of imposter syndrome. It takes focused dedication. AND no one throws you a parade after you get the sucker written! The excitement I had of achieving the goal of writing my own book quickly shifted into depression. I was in the thick of it and didn't know why. I tried to figure it out and wasn't getting anywhere, so I phoned my friend, Diana. She was the perfect person to call.

Without hesitation, she was there for me. She listened. She asked questions. She discovered what I was thinking, feeling, and the stories I was telling myself. She knew exactly what to say. She knew what to say because she listened to her heart and intuition and let it guide her. She encouraged me and did her best to uplift my spirts. She also did a very wise thing; she gave me an assignment.

Diana told me to get a piece of paper and write down three things.

1. Why am I feeling the way I'm feeling?

2. Why am I feeling the way I'm feeling?

3. Why am I feeling the way I'm feeling?

She said answer each question, then meditate and answer the same question five more times. She said taking this action will surface what's at the bottom of the depression. Then she said, "Call me when you're done."

She was absolutely right! I called Diana after I finished and told her I had discovered the reason I was depressed. It was because I wanted someone to tell me I had written a good book. It was all about validation, acceptance and approval from others.

She asked me another question, "Why did you write this book?" At the end of our call, I knew that my book was about more than acceptance and approval. My book was about something bigger than me – it was about developing something to help someone else.

When you're seeking validation from others, you can be defeated by one simple negative post on social media or a poor book review on Amazon. When you know your book, your art, your gift was generously created to help others, no one can take that away from you.

My book was also written so that my children would know at any point in their lives, no matter what their age, they can pursue and accomplish their dreams. This, again, is a truth no one can take away from me – even a nasty book reviewer!

If you're stuck and in the thick of darkness,
    take action to move towards the light.

Two years ago, I had the opportunity to travel to South Africa to speak at a conference. One of the people who I discovered in Johannesburg was Atrayah. I saw her during the reception the night before the conference began. I couldn't help but notice her from across the room. Even though she was small in stature, she was beaming with beautiful light. I introduced myself to her and we had an instant connection, because we made eye contact, smiled, and let our guards down. We were vulnerable with each other. We started asking questions and listening to each other. We were engaged. It was a perfect moment of connection.

The next day, after my keynote, she motioned for me to come to her table. As we sat together, the connection continued to build. She started talking about energy in a way I had never heard anyone talk before. She explained she could see my energy connecting with each person in the room and bouncing from one person to the next, connecting people to me and to each other. She said my energy had been there before. She was talking so profoundly that my mind couldn't keep up. My soul knew what she was saying, but my mind couldn't completely grasp the message. I felt like a kindergardener next to a very wise woman. Remember, I work at a National Laboratory where brilliant scientists talk about energy almost every day! I later learned that she works for Arch Bishop Desmond Tutu. No wonder she is so wise, deep and spiritual!

She had been doing a lot of mentoring and helping others by sharing her story, but had only talked with people one-on-one. Do you think a person like that might have the potential to influence a whole room full of people? Obviously! She has an amazing story and amazing energy.

I told her she should be a speaker and tell her story. It turns out she doesn't have any problem getting up in front of people to speak and could see herself doing it. She just had never considered it before.

What I did for her by making the decision to walk across the room to meet her was to create the opportunity for a connection, discover who she was, and then inspire her to share her value with others.

Some people may think that having an inner circle is all about them and their dreams. If you look at an inner circle as only how people can serve you, then you're really going to undermine the truest meaning of an inner circle. An inner circle is a way for you to discover your greatest potential by showing up to serve and mentor others.

How do you do that? You go through an act of discovery.

I came to understand who Atrayah was and saw the value in her. Even though I felt like a kindergardener compared to her, I had something to offer as a mentor the same as she did to me. I had a profound insight to offer her that could've very well been life changing for her.

"There is no paycheck that can equal the feeling of contentment that comes from being the person you are meant to be."
~ Oprah Winfrey

I've learned that our biggest reward won't come from the stage, a paycheck, book reviews, book sales, or any level of demand and status. Our biggest reward will be those moments that aren't in front of anyone: the moments when only one or two people know about them; the moments when we had the courage and willingness to serve another human being.

There are so many more similar stories. It's in these divine moments when you know you are on this earth for a reason and that reason is to help others. This is what keeps me going, even when I'm tired and stressed. Knowing I am making a difference is what feeds and enriches my soul. We're each on this planet for a reason. You are on this planet for a reason. What is your greatest potential? How could the world be richer, better, and healthier because of your gifts?

Begin discovering those around you, build your inner circle and then you, too, will discover your greatest potential!

CHAPTER**THIRTEEN**

Staring Down the Biggest Mean Girl of All!

We all know this girl. She's been with us our entire lives. She's the one who looks back at us from the mirror each morning and fills our minds and hearts with lies and negative stories about us and causes us to believe our lives don't have meaning, and we don't matter. She fools us into thinking we aren't good enough; our talents aren't valuable, and our contributions are lame. Doubt and negativity silence our voices, make us feel insecure about our talents and gifts, and cons us into thinking we don't matter. As a result, we're paralyzed, depressed and in a sea of darkness.

Have you been there? Do you know what I'm talking about?

At this very moment in time, my *mean girl* is a raging b*#%&! As I'm writing this last chapter, my inner *mean girl* is yelling:

You don't matter!

Who do you think you are?

Who are you to write this book?

People are going to laugh at you and mock you.

You aren't good enough!

I feel I've been beaten up; my energy is low; I'm drained from the verbal abuse and from battling this negative *mean girl*.

On the way home from work, I phoned a friend, with what felt like my last life line. She listened, she reminded me that I'm not alone, and that all women have inner *mean girls*. She encouraged me by telling me that what I have to offer is valuable and the pain of this inner *mean girl* is exactly why I need to write this book. Her positive comments and support moved me further away from the cliff of doubt.

When I got home, my husband embraced me with a warm hug. His genuine affection instantly brought tears to my eyes. He asked me, "What's wrong, babe?" My response, "I don't feel good about myself. My confidence is shattered." He hugged me again and said something silly that caused me to laugh.

Isn't it crazy how much angst our inner *mean girl* can create?

Can you imagine putting up with anyone
saying these lies to you,
or yelling at you this way?
Then, why do you allow yourself to talk this way?

The inner *mean girl* is a huge ugly monster! You know what that means? That means there's also a huge powerhouse of a woman inside of you just begging to get out and confront this *mean girl*.

You can handle an inner *mean girl* in two ways:

1. Show compassion and love by mentoring your *mean girl*

Just like the other *mean girls* you've encountered, there's a reason for her negative behavior. She has feelings of doubt and inadequacy. She's targeting you to make herself feel better. If your inner *mean girl* can convince you that you aren't enough, she'll win. She tells you that failure and risk need to be avoided at all cost; and there's nothing wrong with staying safe in your comfort zone. If you believe her, you'll stop chasing your dreams and stop driving towards your calling and purpose in life. Instead, you'll buy into the latest new Netflix series with a glass of wine and chocolates close at hand. You'll be able to justify it all because, after all, you weren't good enough to go after your dreams and you didn't want to get hurt and ruin your reputation. Right?

This is such an easy trap to fall into. It's much easier to succumb to the negative beliefs than to fight the battles of blazing a trail that hadn't existed before you.

Remind yourself that when you're chasing after a dream and doing something new in life, it's normal to have uncertainty and doubt. That's part of life. Failure is also part of life. Don't let the fear of failure hold you back. No one likes to fail, but it's the only way we grow. That's worth repeating. Failure is the only way we grow. Think about it for a moment. When was the last time you grew without failing?

Children are masters at this – think of a little 12-month-old baby who is learning to walk. He falls down over and over and over again. He doesn't give up, become insecure and hide in a corner or have a nervous breakdown over it! He simply gets back up and tries again, falls and tries again, falls and tries again and again. Soon he is walking, jumping and running just as you will by falling, trying and trying again and then becoming an overnight success!

What does it mean to fail? It means you'll grow! Failing is what will help you learn and grow. Most women are afraid to fail because of a scarcity mindset that there's not enough opportunities for women and there's so few seats for women at the table. With a scarcity mindset, we can't grow and become what we want to become, do and have in life.

It's this toxic scarcity mindset that keeps women competing for the shortage of seats at the table instead of building a bigger table with more seats. We need to stop believing this myth of scarcity and lack. This belief that there's not enough opportunity, not enough love, not enough whatever is a myth! The only thing that there's a lack of is enough women coming together to create opportunities and build a bigger table. Every time a group of women get fired up, watch out because that's when big things happen!

Failures won't kill you – they will redirect you and may send you on a different path, but it will be the path you need to take. Failure is an opportunity to reassess. Learn from it. Embrace it. Then, begin again renewed, stronger and wiser. No one expects you to master a new skill the first time you're attempting it. Give yourself some grace. No one, that is, except your inner *mean girl!*

I began speaking in 2010. That was almost 10 years ago AND rejection still hurts all these years later. Yet, it's part of the business of a professional speaker.

I told you earlier in the book about my mastermind group, which is made up of women professional speakers. We talk every other week and whenever one of us gets a "No, thank you" to a proposal, we share it with each other. Don't get me wrong, we share plenty of success stories, too, but my point is that we share because we need our inner circle to rally around us and remind us how valuable we are and the positive difference we're making in this world. We need it because even though we've been told plenty of times that we're great speakers, when we're dealing with rejection, we aren't feeling so great.

Without fail, the members of the mastermind group are immediately there to support each other. We listen, we ask questions, and we provide clarity, encouragement and lift each other up out of the rejection. We also celebrate each other's victories with complete sincerity.

"The only way forward
is for women to actually support,
celebrate, and champion each other.
Because otherwise, this stuff
is going to stay the same.
Nothing is ever going to change
unless we actually change our approach."
~ Abby Wambach.

2. Silence your inner *mean girl* **and the negativity with positivity**

Imagine that your inner *mean girl* is your friend. What would you say to a friend who was rambling on and on about her shortcomings, fears and doubts? You'd encourage her and point out all her strengths, right? This is exactly what you need to do with your inner *mean girl*. Think of her as a close friend who you need to love and mentor and fill with positive truth.

One of the ways I do this is through my daily ritual of a morning meditation, prayer, visioning exercise, positive affirmations and journaling. Each morning I spend 10-30 minutes in this ritual, and it prepares me for the day. It arms me for challenges. It fills up my heart and mind with positive energy, drive and a deliberate approach to the day.

Surround yourself with positive people. The worst thing you can do when you're depressed is reach out to a friend who is usually depressed and down on herself. Why? Because she's running on empty and doesn't have any positivity to give.

Be cautious about who you spend the most time with and who you reach out to in moments of weakness.

Take some time for self-reflection and ask yourself a few questions:

- What is my truth about this moment?
- What are the facts about this moment?
- What do I need to learn in this moment?
- Why is this happening to me?
- What is this teaching me?

Shift your mindset from:

~~Why is this happening to me?~~

To:

What is this teaching me?

Answering these questions will help you move out of a negative mindset and into discovering your truth and what you can learn from that moment. When this happens, thank God for it! With each of these learning moments, we grow and move into the women we were meant to become.

All too often, we get wrapped up in negativity about not hitting a goal by a particular date. That goal may have been earning a six-figure salary, being promoted with a fancy title, being married to the man of your dreams, living in your dream home, having a child or children or being at your ideal weight. Our inner *mean girl* can come on strong when we miss a goal with a deadline.

First of all, know that if you actually set goals and write them down with a due date, you're part of a limited percentage of the human population. In fact, according to a Harvard University study, less than 3% of the population write down their goals and assign a due date. Pat yourself on the shoulder for being part of this elite 3%. If you actually write down your goals, you have a 50% greater chance of achieving them. If you want to turn the invisible into the visible, you must keep going. So, you miss a deadline – so what!

Pay attention to your purpose, go through the self-reflection process, reevaluate your goal, make it vividly clear and assign a new deadline. Stay focused!

What keeps you focused is your priorities, goals and values. This is why having your goals, values and mission statement written down is so important. This is what will make your choices easier. This is what will be your guide when you make choices in the moment based on what's all around you. This is what will keep you strong when your inner *mean girl* comes knocking.

There are times when we veer away from our goals because of personal situations in our lives. If you have a goal of writing a book by a certain date and that date comes and goes because you were busy raising your children or getting your business off the ground, don't beat yourself up about it. What's important is that you have a goal and you're moving forward.

It's not about how fast you run,
it's about finishing the race.

> You need to learn to fight for your own life and create
> your own path. I want to be more of a voice to inspire
> women and I need you to join me. We need to come
> together and tell women they can live the lives they
> want to live, and it's okay to make the choice to go after
> their dreams. I want women to know they don't need to
> live a life less than they are, want or deserve. Instead
> of being afraid to take risks, lean into the risks and fail
> big! If you want the big win, you've got to be willing
> to fail big! Listen, if you stay in the game and keep
> moving forward, you'll get the goal. It may not happen
> on the timeline you have planned, but you'll hit the
> goal. It's only a matter of time and persistence. If that
> means you need to tell your inner *mean girl* to shut the
> H#*& up – do it!
>
> We need to come together as women and champion
> each other. We must develop the mindset of Ubuntu
> and believe when one woman wins, we all win. I get
> it. We each want to win. We each want the accolades.
> But, the truth is we'll be better if we're all winning,
> instead of only one of us.

I developed a highly competitive spirit at a young age.
What I've learned is women who are wise, healthy,
strong and confident, compete ***with*** other women to
raise their game – NOT ***against*** each other!
We've got to lift each other up!
This is how we collectively rise!

> We can create our own destiny, our own futures, and it
> will require a mindset of abundance. We can move past

the limitations that we and the women's culture have placed on ourselves. We can create something new, something better than where we are today. We need more women to join in the revolution to shift the culture of women and start believing in an abundance mindset and in a culture where we lift each other up by celebrating each woman after a big win or lifting her up after a big fall. Your legacy will not be about your greatest victories, it will be about what you did for other people.

One of the things I'm constantly telling people, especially women, is that they are leaders and should stop pretending they are less powerful and influential than they actually are! Leadership isn't about position. It's about behavior. All of us can be leaders and we can contribute wherever we find ourselves.

I love how Abby Wambach described leadership. She said:

"Leadership is not a position to earn

It's an inherit power to claim

Leadership is the blood that

runs through our veins

It's born in you

It's not the privilege of a few

It's the right and responsibility of all

Leadership is not a right that the world gives to you

It's an offering that you give to the world"

Show yourself some grace, just as you would your best friend. I encourage you to stay on track as best you can while you're living your life. If you need to take a detour and readjust your timeline, do it. Don't give up. Continue your journey and move forward. You'll get where you want to go…one step at a time, in your right time.

That is exactly my goal. In the beginning, this book didn't even have a chapter on *mean girl* behavior and now it's on the cover page. I thought I knew what I wanted to write about but as I began writing, the *mean girl* concept kept coming to me. I hadn't planned on writing a book for women and as I wrote, it became abundantly clear that was exactly what I needed to write. I started reaching out to women and asking them for their stories. Every woman I talked with had a story and most were emotional as they recalled the experience of their personal *mean girl* story.

I don't know if epidemic is the right label. What I do know is that this negative behavior is rampant, it's been happening for decades and is still happening all too often! What I also know is that women are powerful, especially when they come together. Have you experienced the power of women coming together over a common situation? Have you experienced the power of women who are united? Have you experienced the power of love and support amongst a group of women? It's the most beautiful and powerful experience on the planet.

Will you join me in this journey to create positive change? A movement begins with one person. If you join me, there will be at least two of us. . .

When women support each other,
Incredible things happen.

Imagine how much more successful you'd be with an inner circle. Imagine how much more relationship capital you'd have. Imagine creating the life and the career you've always wanted where you could shine and bring your brightest self to the table each day.

You have untapped potential that you haven't yet realized. How do you realize it?

Stop being passive observers of your lives. You have gifts you can offer others. Go through an active process of discovery, form your inner circle, and then, not only will there be people to support you, but you'll realize your greatest potential of all by being there for other people!

I love what Rachel Hollis says, "Someone else's opinion is none of your business, and that nobody else gets to tell you who to be." In her journey, she has and continues to be challenged to keep spreading this message. She still experiences fear. She chooses to show up and practice courage in the face of fear.

The number one way to keep your inner *mean girl* at bay is to surround yourself with a positive inner circle: an inner circle who can nurture you, pick you up and hold you with compassion; an inner circle who can make you laugh when you want to bawl like a baby; an inner circle who gets you, understands your challenges and provides you with the prefect advice and encouragement you need to get out of the funk of the negative *mean girl* valley and back up where you belong.

Please remember. . .

there's always someone who needs to hear your story. . . always, always, always.

My prayer is that someone is you.

With love,

Peggy

About Peggy Vasquez

Peggy works with Administrative Professionals, Managers, Human Resources and Conference Planners. She provides coaching and training for administrative professionals to increase their communication, partnerships and professionalism so they can make more money, get more work done and be happier at work on a daily basis.

Peggy is known internationally for her inspirational keynotes. She's in high-demand as a keynote speaker, she's a relationship expert, a trainer and coach. For over a decade, Peggy's focused and worked in personal development. Peggy is also the author of *NOT, Just An Admin!* Her passion and personal mission statement is to empower others to succeed and that is exactly what she'll do for you. She'll share knowledge and experience from over 25 years in the administrative profession, entertain you with humor and inspire you through passion.

Peggy has provided training programs to administrative assistants at some of the world's most recognized companies including Facebook, Microsoft, Boeing, Vanderbilt, Bath-Fitter, Webcor and many more.

She is actively involved in her community including the Past President of Women Helping Women and is the Founder and Past President of the Administrative Professionals of Tri-Cities. Peggy has been the Chief Executive Assistant at Pacific Northwest National Laboratory since 2005, is a certified trainer and certified Professional Executive Assistant. When Peggy isn't working she can be found with her family, husband on the dance floor or the card table where she's a fierce competitor!

Her most successful accomplishment is being married to her husband, Renè for over 30 years and raising four children and spoiling seven grandchildren together!